UK Boutique Air Fryer Cookbook 2024

2377 Days Air Fryer Recipes From crunchy appetizers to decadent desserts, it's all the way to the top.

Ila T. Fuller

CONTENTS

Beef & Lamb And Pork Recipes 43

Vegetarian & Vegan Recipes 77

Desserts Recipes 90

Recipe Index 101

Introduction

In recent years, the kitchen appliance market has witnessed a revolutionary addition that has transformed the way we cook – the Air Fryer. This compact and versatile device has gained immense popularity for its ability to prepare delicious and crispy meals with significantly less oil compared to traditional frying methods. In this comprehensive guide, we will delve into the advantages of using an Air Fryer, share essential cooking techniques, and provide insights into the proper cleaning and maintenance to ensure longevity and optimal performance.

Unlocking the Advantages of Air Fryers

1 Health Benefits

One of the primary reasons behind the Air Fryer's rising popularity is its health-conscious approach. By utilizing hot air circulation technology, it enables cooking with up to 75% less oil, reducing unhealthy fat intake while maintaining the crispy texture of your favorite dishes.

2 Time Efficiency

Air Fryers boast impressive cooking times, often faster than traditional methods. The rapid hot air circulation ensures that your meals are cooked evenly and quickly, making it an ideal appliance for busy individuals seeking efficiency in the kitchen.

3 Versatility

From frying to baking, roasting to grilling, Air Fryers offer a wide range of cooking options in a single appliance. This versatility makes it a must-have for those looking to experiment with diverse culinary creations.

4 Energy Efficiency

Compared to conventional ovens, Air Fryers consume less energy, contributing to a more sustainable and eco-friendly cooking process. The reduced cooking times also play a role in minimizing energy consumption.

Mastering the Art of Air Frying

1 Preheating

Preheating your Air Fryer is crucial for achieving optimal results. This step ensures that the hot air circulates evenly, leading to consistent and thoroughly cooked dishes.

2 Choosing the Right Temperature

Understanding the appropriate temperature for different dishes is key to successful air frying. The guide will explore temperature ranges for various foods, ensuring that you achieve the perfect balance between crispiness and tenderness.

3 Proper Basket Arrangement

Arranging food items in the Air Fryer basket requires strategic placement to allow even cooking. This section will provide insights into organizing your ingredients for the best results.

4 Using Oil Wisely

While Air Fryers significantly reduce the need for oil, using the right type and amount can enhance the flavor and texture of your dishes. This chapter will cover smart oil choices and application techniques.

5 Exploring Seasonings and Marinades

Elevate your air-fried meals by experimenting with various seasonings and marinades. Discover the perfect combinations to add flavor and personality to your dishes.

Cleaning and Maintaining Your Air Fryer

1 Regular Cleaning Routine

Maintaining cleanliness is crucial for the longevity of your Air Fryer. Learn step-by-step instructions for cleaning the basket, tray, and other components to prevent the buildup of residue.

2 Deep Cleaning Tips

In-depth cleaning is necessary to ensure that all parts of the Air Fryer remain in top condition. This chapter will guide you through the process of disassembling and cleaning hard-to-reach areas.

3 Avoiding Common Pitfalls

Discover common mistakes that can impact the performance of your Air Fryer and learn how to avoid them. This section aims to troubleshoot issues and offer solutions for a seamless cooking experience.

4 Extending Longevity Through Maintenance

Proper maintenance is key to ensuring your Air Fryer lasts for years. From checking electrical components to handling mechanical parts, this chapter provides insights into maintaining your appliance's overall health.

Breakfast & Snacks And Fries Recipes
French Toast Slices

Servings: 1

Ingredients:

- 2 eggs
- 5 slices sandwich bread
- 100ml milk
- 2 tbsp flour
- 3 tbsp sugar
- 1 tsp ground cinnamon
- 1/2 tsp vanilla extract
- Pinch of salt

Directions:

1. Preheat your air fryer to 220ºC
2. Take your bread and cut it into three pieces of the same size
3. Take a mixing bowl and combine the other ingredients until smooth
4. Dip the bread into the mixture, coating evenly
5. Take a piece of parchment paper and lay it inside the air fryer
6. Arrange the bread on the parchment paper in one layer
7. Cook for 5 minutes
8. Turn and cook for another 5 minutes

Morning Sausage Wraps

Servings: 8

Ingredients:

- 8 sausages, chopped into pieces
- 2 slices of cheddar cheese, cut into quarters
- 1 can of regular crescent roll dough
- 8 wooden skewers

Directions:

1. Take the dough and separate each one
2. Cut open the sausages evenly
3. The one of your crescent rolls and on the widest part, add a little sausage and then a little cheese
4. Roll the dough and tuck it until you form a triangle
5. Repeat this for four times and add into your air fryer
6. Cook at 190ºC for 3 minutes
7. Remove your dough and add a skewer for serving
8. Repeat with the other four pieces of dough

Breakfast Doughnuts

Servings: 4

Ingredients:

- 1 packet of Pillsbury Grands
- 5 tbsp raspberry jam
- 1 tbsp melted butter
- 5 tbsp sugar

Directions:

1. Preheat your air fryer to 250°C
2. Place the Pillsbury Grands into the air fryer and cook for around 5m minutes
3. Remove and place to one side
4. Take a large bowl and add the sugar
5. Coat the doughnuts in the melted butter, coating evenly
6. Dip into the sugar and coat evenly once more
7. Using an icing bag, add the jam into the bag and pipe an even amount into each doughnut
8. Eat warm or cold

Healthy Stuffed Peppers

Servings: 2

Ingredients:

- 1 large bell pepper, deseeded and cut into halves
- 1 tsp olive oil
- 4 large eggs
- Salt and pepper to taste

Directions:

1. Take your peppers and rub a little olive oil on the edges
2. Into each pepper, crack one egg and season with salt and pepper
3. You will need to insert a trivet into your air fryer to hold the peppers, and then arrange the peppers evenly
4. Set your fryer to 200°C and cook for 13 minutes
5. Once cooked, remove and serve with a little more seasoning, if required

Hard Boiled Eggs Air Fryer Style

Servings: 2

Ingredients:

- 4 large eggs
- 1 tsp cayenne pepper
- Salt and pepper for seasoning

Directions:

1. Preheat the air fryer to 220°C
2. Take a wire rack and place inside the air fryer
3. Lay the eggs on the rack
4. Cook for between 15-17 minutes, depending upon how you like your eggs
5. Remove from the fryer and place in a bowl of cold water for around 5 minutes
6. Peel and season with the cayenne and the salt and pepper

Delicious Breakfast Casserole

Servings: 4

Ingredients:

- 4 frozen hash browns
- 8 sausages, cut into pieces
- 4 eggs
- 1 diced yellow pepper
- 1 diced green pepper
- 1 diced red pepper
- Half a diced onion

Directions:

1. Line the bottom of your fryer with aluminium foil and arrange the hash browns inside
2. Add the sausage on top (uncooked)
3. Now add the onions and the peppers, sprinkling evenly
4. Cook the casserole on 170°C for around 10 minutes
5. Open your fryer and give the mixture a good stir
6. Combine the eggs in a small bowl and pour over the casserole, closing the lid
7. Cook for another 10 minutes on the same temperature
8. Serve with a little seasoning to taste

European Pancakes

Servings: 5

Ingredients:

- 3 large eggs
- 130g flour
- 140ml whole milk
- 2 tbsp unsweetened apple sauce
- A pinch of salt

Directions:

1. Set your fryer to 200°C and add five ramekins inside to heat up
2. Place all your ingredients inside a blender to combine
3. Spray the ramekins with a little cooking spray
4. Pour the batter into the ramekins carefully
5. Fry for between 6-8 minutes, depending on your preference
6. Serve with your favourite toppings

Cheesy Sausage Breakfast Pockets

Servings: 2

Ingredients:

- 1 packet of regular puff pastry
- 4 sausages, cooked and crumbled into pieces
- 5 eggs
- 50g cooked bacon
- 50g grated cheddar cheese

Directions:

1. Scramble your eggs in your usual way
2. Add the sausage and the bacon as you are cooking the eggs and combine well
3. Take your pastry sheets and cut rectangular shapes
4. Add a little of the egg and meat mixture to one half of each pastry piece
5. Fold the rectangles over and use a fork to seal down the edges
6. Place your pockets into your air fryer and cook at 190°C for 10 minutes
7. Allow to cool before serving

Your Favourite Breakfast Bacon

Servings: 2

Ingredients:

- 4-5 rashers of lean bacon, fat cut off
- Salt and pepper for seasoning

Directions:

1. Line your air fryer basket with parchment paper
2. Place the bacon in the basket
3. Set the fryer to 200°C
4. Cook for 10 minutes for crispy. If you want it very crispy, cook for another 2 minutes

Loaded Hash Browns

Servings: 4

Ingredients:

- 4 large potatoes
- 2 tbsp bicarbonate of soda
- 1 tbsp salt
- 1 tbsp black pepper
- 1 tsp cayenne pepper
- 2 tbsp olive oil
- 1 large chopped onion
- 1 chopped red pepper
- 1 chopped green pepper

Directions:

1. Grate the potatoes
2. Squeeze out any water contained within the potatoes
3. Take a large bowl of water and add the potatoes
4. Add the bicarbonate of soda, combine everything and leave to soak for 25 minutes
5. Drain the water away and carefully pat the potatoes to dry
6. Transfer your potatoes into another bowl
7. Add the spices and oil
8. Combining everything well, tossing to coat evenly
9. Place your potatoes into your fryer basket
10. Set to 200°C and cook for 10 minutes
11. Give the potatoes a shake and add the peppers and the onions
12. Cook for another 10 minutes

Oozing Baked Eggs

Servings: 2

Ingredients:

- 4 eggs
- 140g smoked gouda cheese, cut into small pieces
- Salt and pepper to taste

Directions:

1. You will need two ramekin dishes and spray each one before using
2. Crack two eggs into each ramekin dish
3. Add half of the Gouda cheese to each dish
4. Season and place into the air fryer
5. Cook at 350ºC for 15 minutes, until the eggs are cooked as you like them

Sauces & Snack And Appetiser Recipes
Air Fryer Baked Egg Cups W Spinach & Cheese

Servings: 1

Cooking Time: 10 Mints

Ingredients:

- 1 large (1 large) egg
- 1 tablespoon milk or half & half
- 1 tablespoon frozen spinach , thawed (or sautéed fresh spinach)
- 1-2 teaspoons grated cheese
- salt , to taste
- black pepper, to taste
- Cooking Spray, for muffin cups or ramekins

Directions:

1. Spray inside of silicone muffin cups or ramekin with oil spray. Add egg, milk, spinach and cheese into the muffin cup or ramekin.

2. Add salt, pepper or seasonings to the egg. Gently stir ingredients into egg whites without breaking the yolk.

3. Air Fry at 330°F/165°C for about 6-12 minutes (single egg cups usually take about 6 minutes – multiple or doubled up cups take as much as 12. As you add more egg cups, you will need to add more time.)

4. Timing Note: Cooking in a ceramic ramekin may take a little longer. If you want runny yolks, cook for less time. Keep checking the eggs after 5 minutes to ensure the egg is to your preferred texture.

Air Fryer Frozen Jalapeno Poppers

Servings: 2
Cooking Time: 8 Mints
Ingredients:

- 6 Frozen Jalapeño Poppers

Directions:

1. Place the frozen jalapeño poppers in the air fryer basket and spread out evenly in a single layer. No oil spray is needed.
2. Air Fry at 380°F/193°C for 5 minutes. Gently shake or turn. Continue to Air Fry at 380°F/193°C for another 2-4 minutes or until the cheese just starts to ooze out.
3. Make sure to let them cool a little before eating. The filling can be super hot.

Wholegrain Pitta Chips

Servings: 2
Ingredients:

- 2 round wholegrain pittas, chopped into quarters
- 1 teaspoon olive oil
- ½ teaspoon garlic salt

Directions:

1. Preheat the air-fryer to 200ºC/400ºF.
2. Pop the pittas into the preheated air-fryer and air-fry for 1 minute.
3. Remove the pittas from the air-fryer and spread a layer of the passata/strained tomatoes on the pittas, then scatter over the mozzarella, oregano and oil. Return to the air-fryer and air-fry for a further 4 minutes. Scatter over the basil leaves and serve immediately.

Onion Pakoda

Servings: 2

Ingredients:

- 200g gram flour
- 2 onions, thinly sliced
- 1 tbsp crushed coriander seeds
- 1 tsp chilli powder
- ¾ tsp salt
- ¼ tsp turmeric
- ¼ tsp baking soda

Directions:

1. Mix all the ingredients together in a large bowl
2. Make bite sized pakodas
3. Heat the air fryer to 200ºC
4. Line the air fryer with foil
5. Place the pakoda in the air fryer and cook for 5 minutes
6. Turn over and cook for a further 5 minutes

Air Fryer Sausages

Servings: 6

Cooking Time: 10-15 Mints

Ingredients:

- 6 sausages of your choice

Directions:

1. Pierce the sausages a few times all over using a sharp knife (this is optional, but will help release more fat). Arrange the sausages in a single layer in an air fryer basket.
2. Set the air fry to 180°C/350°F and cook for 10-15 mins, turning every 5 mins, until the sausages are cooked through. If you have a meat thermometer, check they have reached 74°C/165°F in the middle. Serve as a side for breakfast or in buns.

Corn Nuts

Servings: 8

Ingredients:

- 1 giant white corn
- 3 tbsp vegetable oil
- 2 tsp salt

Directions:

1. Place the corn in a large bowl, cover with water and sit for 8 hours
2. Drain, pat dry and air dry for 20 minutes
3. Preheat the air fryer to 200°C
4. Place in a bowl and coat with oil and salt
5. Cook in the air fryer for 10 minutes shake then cook for a further 10 minutes

Air Fryer French Toast Sticks

Servings: 6

Cooking Time: 5 Mints

Ingredients:

- 2 large eggs
- 80 ml double cream
- 80 ml whole milk
- 3 tbsp. caster sugar
- 1/4 tsp. ground cinnamon
- 1/2 tsp. vanilla extract
- Salt
- 6 thick slices white loaf or brioche, each slice cut into thirds
- Maple syrup, for serving

Directions:

1. Beat eggs, cream, milk, sugar, cinnamon, vanilla, and a pinch of salt in a large shallow baking dish. Add bread, turn to coat a few times.
2. Arrange french toast in a basket of air fryer, working in batches as necessary to not overcrowd basket. Set air fryer to 190°C/375°F and cook until golden, about 8 minutes, tossing halfway through.
3. Serve toast warm, drizzled with maple syrup

Air-fried Pickles

Servings: 4

Ingredients:

- 1/2 cup mayonnaise
- 2 tsp sriracha sauce
- 1 jar dill pickle slices
- 1 egg
- 2 tbsp milk
- 50g flour
- 50g cornmeal
- ½ tsp seasoned salt
- ¼ tsp paprika
- ¼ tsp garlic powder
- ⅛ tsp pepper
- Cooking spray

Directions:

1. Mix the mayo and sriracha together in a bowl and set aside
2. Heat the air fryer to 200ºC
3. Drain the pickles and pat dry
4. Mix egg and milk together, in another bowl mix all the remaining ingredients
5. Dip the pickles in the egg mix then in the flour mix
6. Spray the air fryer with cooking spray
7. Cook for about 4 minutes until crispy

Air Fryer Scalloped Potatoes

Servings: 3-4
Cooking Time: 40 Mints

Ingredients:

- 454 g potatoes , washed and dried (about 3 medium potatoes)
- oil spray
- 180 ml heavy cream
- 1/2 teaspoon salt, or to taste
- 1/4 teaspoon garlic powder
- 1/4 teaspoon black pepper
- 57 g shredded cheddar cheese

Directions:

1. Peel and slice potatoes thin and spray oil evenly over the potatoes.
2. Spray the inside bottom and sides of the cake pan with oil. Lay the potato slices in a neat stack with their edges aligned vertically into the prepared bucket pan. Fan the potatoes out if there is room after they are in the bucket pan. Place the pan into the Air Fryer.
3. Air Fry at 360°F/180°C for an initial 18 minutes.
4. Combine heavy cream, salt, garlic powder and black pepper. Stir until well combined.
5. After the potatoes have air fried for the initial 18 minutes, pour the cream mixture over the potatoes. Spread cream over potatoes and gently press the potatoes down to help them settle into the cream.
6. Air Fry the potatoes again with the cream mixture at reduced temperature of 300°F/150°C for 15-18 minutes, or until potatoes are tender.
7. Sprinkle shredded cheddar cheese over the potatoes. Air Fry at 300°F/150°C for additional 1-2 minutes or until cheese is melted. Allow potatoes to cool for 10 minutes before serving

Mac & Cheese Bites

Servings: 14

Ingredients:

- 200g mac and cheese
- 2 eggs
- 200g panko breadcrumbs
- Cooking spray

Directions:

1. Place drops of mac and cheese on parchment paper and freeze for 1 hour
2. Beat the eggs in a bowl, add the breadcrumbs to another bowl
3. Dip the mac and cheese balls in the egg then into the breadcrumbs
4. Heat the air fryer to 190ºC
5. Place in the air fryer, spray with cooking spray and cook for 15 minutes

Tortellini Bites

Servings: 6

Ingredients:

- 200g cheese tortellini
- 150g flour
- 100g panko bread crumbs
- 50g grated parmesan
- 1 tsp dried oregano
- 2 eggs
- ½ tsp garlic powder
- ½ tsp chilli flakes
- Salt
- Pepper

Directions:

1. Cook the tortellini according to the packet instructions
2. Mix the panko, parmesan, oregano, garlic powder, chilli flakes salt and pepper in a bowl
3. Beat the eggs in another bowl and place the flour in a third bowl
4. Coat the tortellini in flour, then egg and then in the panko mix
5. Place in the air fryer and cook at 185ºC for 10 minutes until crispy
6. Serve with marinara sauce for dipping

Cumin Shoestring Carrots

Servings: 2

Ingredients:

- 300 g/10½ oz. carrots
- 1 teaspoon cornflour/cornstarch
- 1 teaspoon ground cumin
- ¼ teaspoon salt
- 1 tablespoon olive oil
- garlic mayonnaise, to serve

Directions:

1. Preheat the air-fryer to 200ºC/400ºF.
2. Peel the carrots and cut into thin fries, roughly 10 cm x 1 cm x 5 mm/4 x ½ x ¼ in. Toss the carrots in a bowl with all the other ingredients.
3. Add the carrots to the preheated air-fryer and air-fry for 9 minutes, shaking the drawer of the air-fryer a couple of times during cooking. Serve with garlic mayo on the side.

Cheese Wontons

Servings: 8

Ingredients:

- 8 wonton wrappers
- 1 carton pimento cheese
- Small dish of water
- Cooking spray

Directions:

1. Place one tsp of cheese in the middle of each wonton wrapper
2. Brush the edges of each wonton wrapper with water
3. Fold over to create a triangle and seal
4. Heat the air fryer to 190°C
5. Spray the wontons with cooking spray
6. Place in the air fryer and cook for 3 minutes
7. Turnover and cook for a further 3 minutes

Air Fryer White Castle Frozen Sliders

Servings: 3

Cooking Time: 6 Mints

Ingredients:

- 6 frozen White Castle Sliders
- OPTIONAL CONDIMENTS:
- Ketchup, mustard, bbq sauce, pickles , etc

Directions:

1. Do not preheat the air fryer. Using a fork, carefully remove the top bun to expose the meat. Set top bun aside.
2. Place just the bottom bun and patty in the air fryer, meat side up.
3. Air Fry the just the bottom bun with meat and cheese at 340°F/171°C for 5 minutes.
4. Add the top bun to the air fryer next to bottom buns (not on top of). Air fry for 1 minute until top bun is warmed. If you want the slider hotter and crisper, air fry for another 1-2 minutes.
5. Add ketchup, mustard or whatever else you love on your sliders, top with the bun and enjoy!

Air Fryer Frozen Corn Dogs

Servings: 4
Cooking Time: 12 Mints
Ingredients:

- 4 Frozen Corn Dogs

Directions:

1. Place the frozen corn dogs in the air fryer basket and spread out into a single even layer. No oil spray is needed.
2. For Regular sized Corn Dogs: Air Fry at 370°F/188°C for 8 minutes. Flip the corn dogs over and then continue to cook at 370°F/188°C for another 2-4 minutes or until heated through.
3. For Mini sized Corn Dogs: Air Fry at 370°F/188°C for 6 minutes. Gently shake and flip the mini corn dogs over and then continue to cook at 370°F/188°C for another 2-4 minutes or until heated through

Spring Rolls

Servings: 20
Ingredients:

- 160g dried rice noodles
- 1 tsp sesame oil
- 300g minced beef
- 200g frozen vegetables
- 1 onion, diced
- 3 cloves garlic, crushed
- 1 tsp soy sauce
- 1 tbsp vegetable oil
- 1 pack egg roll wrappers

Directions:

1. Soak the noodles in a bowl of water until soft
2. Add the minced beef, onion, garlic and vegetables to a pan and cook for 6 minutes
3. Remove from the heat, stir in the noodles and add the soy
4. Heat the air fryer to 175°C
5. Add a diagonal strip of filling in each egg roll wrapper
6. Fold the top corner over the filling, fold in the two side corners
7. Brush the centre with water and roll to seal
8. Brush with vegetable oil, place in the air fryer and cook for about 8 minutes until browned

Jalapeño Poppers

Servings: 2

Ingredients:

- 10 jalapeños, halved and deseeded
- 100g cream cheese
- 50g parsley
- 150g breadcrumbs

Directions:

1. Mix 1/2 the breadcrumbs with the cream cheese
2. Add the parsley
3. Stuff the peppers with the cream cheese mix
4. Top the peppers with the remaining breadcrumbs
5. Heat the air fryer to 185ºC
6. Place in the air fryer and cook for 6-8 minutes

Jalapeño Pockets

Servings: 4

Ingredients:

- 1 chopped onion
- 60g cream cheese
- 1 jalapeño, chopped
- 8 wonton wrappers
- ¼ tsp garlic powder
- ⅛ tsp onion powder

Directions:

1. Cook the onion in a pan for 5 minutes until softened
2. Add to a bowl and mix with the remaining ingredients
3. Lay the wonton wrappers out and add filling to each one
4. Fold over to create a triangle and seal with water around the edges
5. Heat the air fryer to 200ºC
6. Place in the air fryer and cook for about 4 minutes

Tasty Pumpkin Seeds

Servings: 2

Ingredients:

- 1 ¾ cups pumpkin seeds
- 2 tsp avocado oil
- 1 tsp paprika
- 1 tsp salt

Directions:

1. Preheat air fryer to 180°C
2. Add all ingredients to a bowl and mix well
3. Place in the air fryer and cook for 35 minutes shaking frequently

Plantain Fries

Servings: 2

Ingredients:

- 1 ripe plantain (yellow and brown outside skin)
- 1 teaspoon olive oil
- ¼ teaspoon salt

Directions:

1. Preheat the air-fryer to 180°C/350°F.

2. Peel the plantain and slice into fries about 6 x 1 cm/2½ x ½ in. Toss the fries in oil and salt, making sure every fry is coated.

3. Tip into the preheated air-fryer in a single layer (you may need to cook them in two batches, depending on the size of your air-fryer) and air-fry for 13–14 minutes until brown on the outside and soft on the inside. Serve immediately.

Sweet Potato Crisps

Servings: 4

Ingredients:

- 1 sweet potato, peeled and thinly sliced
- 2 tbsp oil
- ¼ tsp salt
- ¼ tsp pepper
- 1 tsp chopped rosemary
- Cooking spray

Directions:

1. Place all ingredients in a bowl and mix well
2. Place in the air fryer and cook at 175ºC for about 15 minutes until crispy

Bacon Smokies

Servings: 8

Ingredients:

- 150g little smokies (pieces)
- 150g bacon
- 50g brown sugar
- Toothpicks

Directions:

1. Cut the bacon strips into thirds
2. Put the brown sugar into a bowl
3. Coat the bacon with the sugar
4. Wrap the bacon around the little smokies and secure with a toothpick
5. Heat the air fryer to 170ºC
6. Place in the air fryer and cook for 10 minutes until crispy

Poultry Recipes
Grain-free Chicken Katsu

Servings: 4

Ingredients:

- 125 g/1¼ cups ground almonds
- ½ teaspoon salt
- ½ teaspoon garlic powder
- ½ teaspoon dried parsley
- ½ teaspoon freshly ground black pepper
- ¼ teaspoon onion powder
- ¼ teaspoon dried oregano
- 450 g/1 lb. mini chicken fillets
- 1 egg, beaten
- oil, for spraying/drizzling
- coriander/cilantro leaves, to serve
- KATSU SAUCE
- 1 teaspoon olive oil or avocado oil
- 1 courgette/zucchini (approx. 150 g/5 oz.), finely chopped
- 1 carrot (approx. 100 g/3½ oz.), finely chopped
- 1 onion (approx. 120 g/4½ oz.), finely chopped
- 1 eating apple (approx. 150 g/5 oz.), cored and finely chopped
- 1 teaspoon ground ginger
- 1 teaspoon ground turmeric
- 2 teaspoons ground cumin
- 2 teaspoons ground coriander
- 1½ teaspoons mild chilli/chili powder
- 1 teaspoon garlic powder
- 1½ tablespoons runny honey
- 1 tablespoon soy sauce (gluten-free if you wish)
- 700 ml/3 cups vegetable stock (700 ml/3 cups water with 1½ stock cubes)

Directions:

1. First make the sauce. The easiest way to ensure all the vegetables and apple are finely chopped is to combine them in a food processor. Heat the oil in a large saucepan and sauté the finely chopped vegetables and apple for 5 minutes. Add all the seasonings, honey, soy sauce and stock and stir well, then bring to a simmer and simmer for 30 minutes.

2. Meanwhile, mix together the ground almonds, seasonings and spices. Dip each chicken fillet into the beaten egg, then into the almond-spice mix, making sure each fillet is fully coated. Spray the coated chicken fillets with olive oil (or simply drizzle over).

3. Preheat the air-fryer to 180ºC/350ºF.

4. Place the chicken fillets in the preheated air-fryer and air-fry for 10 minutes, turning halfway through cooking. Check the internal temperature of the chicken has reached at least 74ºC/165ºF using a meat thermometer – if not, cook for another few minutes.

5. Blend the cooked sauce in a food processor until smooth. Serve the chicken with the Katsu Sauce drizzled over (if necessary, reheat the sauce gently before serving) and scattered with coriander leaves. Any unused sauce can be frozen.

Air Fryer Fried Chicken

Servings: 3
Cooking Time: 10 Mints
Ingredients:

- 900 g bone-in skin-on chicken pieces (mix of cuts)
- 480 ml buttermilk
- 120 ml hot sauce
- 3 tsp. salt
- 250 g plain flour
- 1 tsp. garlic powder
- 1 tsp. onion powder
- 1/2 tsp. oregano
- 1/2 tsp. freshly ground black pepper
- 1/4 tsp. cayenne pepper

Directions:

1. Trim chicken of excess fat and place in a large bowl. In a medium bowl, combine buttermilk, hot sauce, and 2 teaspoons salt.
2. Pour mixture over chicken, making sure all pieces are coated. Cover and refrigerate for at least 1 hour and up to overnight.
3. In a shallow bowl or pie dish, combine flour, remaining 1 teaspoon salt, and seasonings. Working with one at a time, remove chicken from buttermilk, shaking off excess buttermilk. Place in flour mixture, turning to coat.
4. Place coated chicken in basket of air fryer, working in batches as necessary to not overcrowd the basket. Cook at 200°C/400°F until chicken is golden and internal temperature reaches 73°C/165°F, 20 to 25 minutes, flipping halfway through.
5. Repeat with remaining chicken

Chicken Balls, Greek-style

Servings: 4
Ingredients:

- 500g ground chicken
- 1 egg
- 1 tbsp dried oregano
- 1.5 tbsp garlic paste
- 1 tsp lemon zest
- 1 tsp dried onion powder
- Salt and pepper to taste

Directions:

1. Take a bowl and combine all ingredients well
2. Use your hands to create meatballs - you should be able to make 12 balls
3. Preheat your air fryer to 260ºC
4. Add the meatballs to the fryer and cook for 9 minutes

Air Fryer Turkey Melt

Servings: 1
Cooking Time: 10 Mints
Ingredients:

- 2 slices bread
- Slices leftover turkey slices or deli meat
- 1 Tablespoon butter
- good melting cheese (American, Swiss, cheddar, Gruyere, etc.)

Directions:

1. Layer cheese and turkey slices in between bread. Butter outside of bread with butter. Secure the top slice of bread with toothpicks through the sandwich. Lay sandwich in air fryer basket.
2. Air Fry at 360°F/180°C for about 3-5 minutes to melt the cheese.
3. Flip the sandwich and increase heat to 380°F/180°C to finish and crisp the bread. Air Fry at 380°F/180°C for about 5 minutes or until the sandwich is to your preferred texture. C. Allow it to cool a bit before biting into the yummy grilled cheese sandwich!

Air Fryer Chicken Wings With Honey And Sesame

Servings: 1-2
Cooking Time: 10-30 Mints
Ingredients:

- 450–500g /2 oz chicken wings with tips removed
- 1 tbsp olive oil
- 3 tbsp cornflour
- 1 tbsp runny honey
- 1 tsp soy sauceor tamari
- 1 tsp rice wine vinegar
- 1 tsp toasted sesame oil
- 2 tsp sesame seeds, toasted
- 1 large spring onion, thinly sliced
- salt and freshly ground black pepper

Directions:

1. In a large bowl, toss together the chicken wings, olive oil and a generous amount of salt and pepper. Toss in the cornflour, a tablespoon at a time, until the wings are well coated.
2. Air-fry the chicken wings in a single layer for 25 minutes at 180°C/350°F, turning halfway through the cooking time.
3. Meanwhile, make the glaze by whisking together the honey, soy sauce, rice wine vinegar and toasted sesame oil in a large bowl.
4. Tip the cooked wings into the glaze, tossing until they're well coated. Return to the air fryer in a single layer for 5 more minutes.
5. Toss the wings once more in any remaining glaze. Sprinkle with toasted sesame seeds and spring onion and serve.

Chicken And Cheese Chimichangas

Servings: 6

Ingredients:

- 100g shredded chicken (cooked)
- 150g nacho cheese
- 1 chopped jalapeño pepper
- 6 flour tortillas
- 5 tbsp salsa
- 60g refried beans
- 1 tsp cumin
- 0.5 tsp chill powder
- Salt and pepper to taste

Directions:

1. Take a large mixing bowl and add all of the ingredients, combining well
2. Add ⅓ of the filling to each tortilla and roll into a burrito shape
3. Spray the air fryer with cooking spray and heat to 200°C
4. Place the chimichangas in the air fryer and cook for 7 minutes

Bacon Wrapped Chicken Thighs

Servings: 4

Ingredients:

- 75g softened butter
- ½ clove minced garlic
- ¼ tsp dried thyme
- ¼ tsp dried basil
- ⅛ tsp coarse salt
- 100g thick cut bacon
- 350g chicken thighs, boneless and skinless
- 2 tsp minced garlic
- Salt and pepper to taste

Directions:

1. Take a mixing bowl and add the softened butter, garlic, thyme, basil, salt and pepper, combining well
2. Place the butter onto a sheet of plastic wrap and roll up to make a butter log
3. Refrigerate for about 2 hours
4. Remove the plastic wrap
5. Place one bacon strip onto the butter and then place the chicken thighs on top of the bacon. Sprinkle with garlic
6. Place the cold butter into the middle of the chicken thigh and tuck one end of bacon into the chicken
7. Next, fold over the chicken thigh whilst rolling the bacon around
8. Repeat with the rest
9. Preheat the air fryer to 188C
10. Cook the chicken until white in the centre and the juices run clear

Turkey And Mushroom Burgers

Servings: 2

Ingredients:

- 180g mushrooms
- 500g minced turkey
- 1 tbsp of your favourite chicken seasoning, e.g. Maggi
- 1 tsp onion powder
- 1 tsp garlic powder
- Salt and pepper to taste

Directions:

1. Place the mushrooms in a food processor and puree
2. Add all the seasonings and mix well
3. Remove from the food processor and transfer to a mixing bowl
4. Add the minced turkey and combine again
5. Shape the mix into 5 burger patties
6. Spray with cooking spray and place in the air fryer
7. Cook at 160ºC for 10 minutes, until cooked.

Spicy Chicken Wing Drummettes

Servings: 4

Ingredients:

- 10 large chicken drumettes
- Cooking spray
- 100ml rice vinegar
- 3 tbsp honey
- 2 tbsp unsalted chicken stock
- 1 tbsp lower sodium soy sauce
- 1 tbsp toasted sesame oil
- ⅜ tsp crushed red pepper
- 1 garlic clove, finely chopped
- 2 tbsp chopped, unsalted, roasted peanuts
- 1 tbsp chopped fresh chives

Directions:

1. Coat the chicken in cooking spray and place inside the air fryer
2. Cook at 200ºC for 30 minutes
3. Take a mixing bowl and combine the vinegar, honey, stock, soy sauce, oil, crushed red pepper and garlic
4. Cook to a simmer, until a syrup consistency is achieved
5. Coat the chicken in this mixture and sprinkle with peanuts and chives

Air Fryer Chicken Drumsticks

Servings: 4
Cooking Time: 25 Mints
Ingredients:

- 8 - 12 chicken drumsticks
- Seasoning
- Oil (optional)

Directions:

1. Preheat the air fryer to 200°C/400°F for 5 minutes.
2. Optionally brush the drumsticks with some oil.
3. Season the chicken drumsticks with your favourite spices. You can just use salt if you prefer.
4. Add the drumsticks to the air fryer basket. You might need to use a trivet to fit them all in, or if you have a smaller air fryer, cook them in batches.
5. Cook for 22 - 25 minutes, turning halfway through.
6. Check the chicken is cooked all the way through - they should reach 75°C/165°F internally, use a meat thermometer if possible.

Chicken Milanese

Servings: 4
Ingredients:

- 130 g/1¾ cups dried breadcrumbs (gluten-free if you wish, see page 9)
- 50 g/⅔ cup grated Parmesan
- 1 teaspoon dried basil
- ½ teaspoon dried thyme
- ¼ teaspoon freshly ground black pepper
- 1 egg, beaten
- 4 tablespoons plain/all-purpose flour (gluten-free if you wish)
- 4 boneless chicken breasts

Directions:

1. Combine the breadcrumbs, cheese, herbs and pepper in a bowl. In a second bowl beat the egg, and in the third bowl have the plain/all-purpose flour. Dip each chicken breast first into the flour, then the egg, then the seasoned breadcrumbs.
2. Preheat the air-fryer to 180°C/350°F.
3. Add the breaded chicken breasts to the preheated air-fryer and air-fry for 12 minutes. Check the internal temperature of the chicken has reached at least 74°C/165°F using a meat thermometer – if not, cook for another few minutes.

Pepper & Lemon Chicken Wings

Servings: 2

Ingredients:

- 1kg chicken wings
- 1/4 tsp cayenne pepper
- 2 tsp lemon pepper seasoning
- 3 tbsp butter
- 1 tsp honey
- An extra 1 tsp lemon pepper seasoning for the sauce

Directions:

1. Preheat the air fryer to 260°C
2. Place the lemon pepper seasoning and cayenne in a bowl and combine
3. Coat the chicken in the seasoning
4. Place the chicken in the air fryer and cook for 20 minutes, turning over halfway
5. Turn the temperature up to 300°C and cook for another 6 minutes
6. Meanwhile, melt the butter and combine with the honey and the rest of the seasoning
7. Remove the wings from the air fryer and pour the sauce over the top

Quick Chicken Nuggets

Servings: 4

Ingredients:

- 500g chicken tenders
- 25g ranch salad dressing mixture
- 2 tbsp plain flour
- 100g breadcrumbs
- 1 egg, beaten
- Olive oil spray

Directions:

1. Take a large mixing bowl and arrange the chicken inside
2. Sprinkle the seasoning over the top and ensure the chicken is evenly coated
3. Place the chicken to one side for around 10 minutes
4. Add the flour into a resealable bag
5. Crack the egg into a small mixing bowl and whisk
6. Pour the breadcrumbs onto a medium sized plate
7. Transfer the chicken into the resealable bag and coat with the flour, giving it a good shake
8. Remove the chicken and dip into the egg, and then rolling it into the breadcrumbs, coating evenly
9. Repeat with all pieces of the chicken
10. Heat your air fryer to 200°C
11. Arrange the chicken inside the fryer and add a little olive oil spray to avoid sticking
12. Cook for 4 minutes, before turning over and cooking for another 4 minutes
13. Remove and serve whilst hot

Cornflake Chicken Nuggets

Servings: 4

Ingredients:

- 100 g/4 cups cornflakes (gluten-free if you wish)
- 70 g/½ cup plus ½ tablespoon plain/all-purpose flour (gluten-free if you wish)
- 2 eggs, beaten
- ½ teaspoon salt
- ¼ teaspoon freshly ground black pepper
- 600 g/1 lb. 5 oz. mini chicken fillets

Directions:

1. Grind the cornflakes in a food processor to a crumb-like texture. Place the flour in one bowl and the beaten eggs in a second bowl; season both bowls with the salt and pepper. Coat each chicken fillet in flour, tapping off any excess. Next dip each flour-coated chicken fillet into the egg, then the cornflakes until fully coated.
2. Preheat the air-fryer to 180ºC/350ºF.
3. Add the chicken fillets to the preheated air-fryer (you may need to add the fillets in two batches, depending on the size of your air-fryer) and air-fry for 10 minutes, turning halfway through cooking. Check the internal temperature of the nuggets has reached at least 74ºC/165ºF using a meat thermometer – if not, cook for another few minutes and then serve.
4. VARIATION: SIMPLE CHICKEN NUGGETS
5. For a simpler version, replace the crushed cornflakes with 90 g/1¼ cups dried breadcrumbs (see page 9). Prepare and air-fry in the same way.

Satay Chicken Skewers

Servings: 4

Ingredients:

- 3 chicken breasts, chopped into 3 x 3-cm/1¼ x 1¼-in. cubes
- MARINADE
- 200 ml/¾ cup canned coconut milk (including the thick part from the can)
- 1 plump garlic clove, finely chopped
- 2 teaspoons freshly grated ginger
- 2 tablespoons soy sauce
- 1 heaped tablespoon peanut butter
- 1 tablespoon maple syrup
- 1 tablespoon mild curry powder
- 1 tablespoon fish sauce

Directions:

1. Mix the marinade ingredients thoroughly in a bowl, then toss in the chopped chicken and stir to coat thoroughly. Leave in the fridge to marinate for at least 4 hours.
2. Preheat the air-fryer to 190ºC/375ºF.
3. Thread the chicken onto 8 metal skewers. Add to the preheated air-fryer (you may need to cook these in two batches, depending on the size of your air-fryer). Air-fry for 10 minutes. Check the internal temperature of the chicken has reached at least 74ºC/165ºF using a meat thermometer – if not, cook for another few minutes and then serve.

Air Fryer Chicken Thighs

Servings: 4
Cooking Time: 12 Mints
Ingredients:

- 454 g skinless chicken thighs
- 3 tablespoons chicken spices
- 2 tablespoons light olive oil

Directions:

1. Preheat air fryer to 400°F/200°C.
2. Pat chicken thighs dry. Drizzle with oil and sprinkle with chicken spices, turn to ensure they are evenly coated with the oil and spice.
3. Place chicken thighs in an air fryer basket in a single layer. Make sure they are not overlapping.
4. Place basket into air fryer and air fry chicken thighs for 12-15 minutes [Note 1], until they are cooked through, and have reached 165°F/ 74°C in the center of the thickest part [Note 2]. Cook for additional 2-3 minute intervals if required until they are done.
5. Remove from the air fryer to a plate, cover with aluminum foil and allow to rest for 5 minutes. This allows the juices to reabsorb ensuring you have juicy tender chicken thighs.

Air Fryer Chicken Schnitzel

Servings: 2

Cooking Time: 10 Mints

Ingredients:

- 1 large chicken breast
- 1 egg
- 2 tablespoons flour
- 147 g breadcrumbs
- ¼ teaspoon garlic powder
- ½ teaspoon salt
- ¼ teaspoon ground black pepper
- Drizzle of light olive oil

Directions:

1. Pat chicken breast dry, then cut in half horizontally through the center.
2. Place the chicken steaks between two pieces of parchment or baking paper, and roll them with a rolling pin until they are around ½ inch thick.
3. Place the breadcrumbs in a large shallow bowl. Mix the flour, garlic powder, salt, and pepper in another large bowl.
4. Place chicken into the flour mixture and toss to coat.
5. Add egg to the bowl with the chicken, split the yolk, and toss to coat.
6. Preheat air fryer to 180°C/360°F.
7. Place each piece of chicken schnitzel into the breadcrumbs, and turn to coat thoroughly. Transfer to a plate, and press the bread crumbs onto the chicken to help them stick.
8. Lightly brush or spritz the chicken schnitzels with oil.
9. Place chicken schnitzels in air fryer basket. Ensure they are not touching. You may need to cook the schnitzels in batches depending on the size of your air fryer.
10. Air fry chicken schnitzels until golden brown and at least 74°C/165°F in the center. This will take approximately 10-12 minutes. Carefully turn the schnitzels halfway through the cooking time if required for your air fryer.

Jerk Chicken

Servings: 8
Cooking Time: 45 Mints
Ingredients:

- 8 chicken leg quarters or chicken drumsticks
- 80 ml apple cider vinegar
- 80 ml dark soy sauce
- 60 ml lime juice
- 120 ml orange juice
- 1 tbsp. allspice
- 1 tsp. black pepper
- 1 tsp. cinnamon
- 2 tsp. fresh thyme
- 3 spring onions, chopped
- 2 tbsp. ginger, peeled and chopped
- 1 medium onion, chopped
- 8 garlic cloves, peeled
- 4 Scotch bonnets, seeds removed

Directions:

1. Pat the skin of your chicken dry and using a knife make small holes all around the chicken.
2. In a blender combine all remaining ingredients and blend for three minutes. Pour half the jerk marinade over the chicken and massage it in. Refrigerate overnight.
3. When ready to cook, bring grill temperature up to 165°C/330°F. Place the chicken skin side down and close BBQ lid for 5-7 minutes until it starts to brown. Turn over and cook for the remaining 5-7 minutes. Repeat twice more until chicken is dark brown and cooked all the way through.
4. Move chicken to the sides of the grill and brush remaining jerk sauce on top. Close the lid and cook for a further 5-7minutes.
5. Remove from BBQ and leave chicken to cool for around 10 minutes. Either eat on the bone or chop the meat into smaller pieces and serve.

Nashville Chicken

Servings: 4

Ingredients:

- 400g boneless chicken breast tenders
- 2 tsp salt
- 2 tsp coarsely ground black pepper
- 2 tbsp hot sauce
- 2 tbsp pickle juice
- 500g all purpose flour
- 3 large eggs
- 300ml buttermilk
- 2 tbsp olive oil
- 6 tbsp cayenne pepper
- 3 tbsp dark brown sugar
- 1 tsp chilli powder
- 1 tsp garlic powder
- 1 tsp paprika
- Salt and pepper to taste

Directions:

1. Take a large mixing bowl and add the chicken, hot sauce, pickle juice, salt and pepper and combine
2. Place in the refrigerator for 3 hours
3. Transfer the flour to a bowl
4. Take another bowl and add the eggs, buttermilk and 1 tbsp of the hot sauce, combining well
5. Press each piece of chicken into the flour and coat well
6. Place the chicken into the buttermilk mixture and then back into the flour
7. Allow to sit or 10 minutes
8. Preheat the air fryer to 193C
9. Whisk together the spices, brown sugar and olive oil to make the sauce and pour over the chicken tenders
10. Serve whilst still warm

Buttermilk Chicken

Servings: 4

Ingredients:

- 500g chicken thighs, skinless and boneless
- 180ml buttermilk
- 40g tapioca flour
- ½ tsp garlic salt
- 1 egg
- 75g all purpose flour
- ½ tsp brown sugar
- 1 tsp garlic powder
- ½ tsp paprika
- ½ tsp onion powder
- ¼ tsp oregano
- Salt and pepper to taste

Directions:

1. Take a medium mixing bowl and combine the buttermilk and hot sauce
2. Add the tapioca flour, garlic salt and black pepper in a plastic bag and shake
3. Beat the egg
4. Take the chicken thighs and tip into the buttermilk, then the tapioca mixture, the egg, and then the flour
5. Preheat air fryer to 190ºC
6. Cook the chicken thighs for 10 minutes, until white in the middle

Air Fryer Rosemary Chicken Breast

Servings: 2

Cooking Time: 20 Mints

Ingredients:

- 2 chicken breasts (1 per person)
- Spray oil
- Salt and pepper
- 1/4 teaspoon smoked paprika
- 1/4 teaspoon garlic salt or garlic powder
- 1 spray of rosemary

Directions:

1. Remove the rosemary leaves from the sprig and chop finely.
2. Add to a bowl with the salt, pepper, garlic powder and a few sprays of oil, or 1/4 teaspoon. Mix well.
3. Brush this mix onto both sides of your chicken breast.
4. Add to the air fryer basket. Cook at 180°C/360°F for 10 minutes.
5. Turn over and spray lightly with oil again if needed.Cook at 180°C/360°F for another 10 minutes.
6. Check that the internal temperature of the rosemary chicken breast is a minimum of 74°C/165°F and then remove from the air fryer.

Honey Cajun Chicken Thighs

Servings: 6

Ingredients:

- 100ml buttermilk
- 1 tsp hot sauce
- 400g skinless, boneless chicken thighs
- 150g all purpose flour
- 60g tapioca flour
- 2.5 tsp cajun seasoning
- ½ tsp garlic salt
- ½ tsp honey powder
- ¼ tsp ground paprika
- ⅛ tsp cayenne pepper
- 4 tsp honey

Directions:

1. Take a large bowl and combine the buttermilk and hot sauce
2. Transfer to a plastic bag and add the chicken thighs
3. Allow to marinate for 30 minutes
4. Take another bowl and add the flour, tapioca flour, cajun seasoning, garlic, salt, honey powder, paprika, and cayenne pepper, combining well
5. Dredge the chicken through the mixture
6. Preheat the air fryer to 175C
7. Cook for 15 minutes before flipping the thighs over and cooking for another 10 minutes
8. Drizzle 1 tsp of honey over each thigh

Beef & Lamb And Pork Recipes
Beef Stroganoff

Servings:4
Cooking Time:20 Minutes
Ingredients:

- 4 cubes / 800 ml beef stock cubes
- 4 tbsp olive oil
- 1 onion, chopped
- 200 g / 7 oz sour cream
- 200 g / 7 oz mushroom, finely sliced
- 500 g / 17.6 oz steak, chopped
- 4 x 100 g / 3.5 oz egg noodles, cooked

Directions:

1. Preheat the air fryer to 200 °C / 400 °F and line the bottom of the basket with parchment paper.
2. Boil 800 ml of water and use it to dissolve the 4 beef stock cubes.
3. In a heat-proof bowl, mix the olive oil, onion, sour cream, mushrooms, and beef stock until fully combined.
4. Coat all sides of the steak chunks in the mixture and set aside to marinate for 10 minutes.
5. Transfer the steak to the air fryer, close the lid, and cook for 10 minutes. Serve the steak hot with a serving of egg noodles.

Air Fryer Roast Pork Belly

Servings: 4
Cooking Time: 55 Mints
Ingredients:

- 1kg piece boneless pork belly, rind scored
- 2 tsp sea salt flakes
- Olive oil spray

Directions:

1. Preheat the air fryer to 200°C/400°F for 3 minutes. Pat pork dry with paper towel. Rub salt into pork rind.
2. Place the pork in the air fryer basket and spray with oil. Set timer for 25 minutes and cook until the rind crackles. Reduce temperature to 160°C/320°F. Set timer for 30 minutes and cook until pork is tender and cooked through

Beef Satay

Servings: 2

Ingredients:

- 400g steak strips
- 2 tbsp oil
- 1 tbsp fish sauce
- 1 tsp sriracha sauce
- 200g sliced coriander (fresh)
- 1 tsp ground coriander
- 1 tbsp soy
- 1 tbsp minced ginger
- 1 tbsp minced garlic
- 1 tbsp sugar
- 25g roasted peanuts

Directions:

1. Add oil, dish sauce, soy, ginger, garlic, sugar sriracha, coriander and ¼ cup coriander to a bowl and mix. Add the steak and marinate for 30 minutes
2. Add the steak to the air fryer and cook at 200ºC for about 8 minutes
3. Place the steak on a plate and top with remaining coriander and chopped peanuts
4. Serve with peanut sauce

Breaded Pork Chops

Servings: 6

Ingredients:

- 6 boneless pork chops
- 1 beaten egg
- 100g panko crumbs
- 75g crushed cornflakes
- 2 tbsp parmesan
- 1 ¼ tsp paprika
- ½ tsp garlic powder
- ½ tsp onion powder
- ¼ tsp chilli powder
- Salt and pepper to taste

Directions:

1. Heat the air fryer to 200ºC
2. Season the pork chops with salt
3. Mix the panko, cornflakes, salt, parmesan, garlic powder, onion powder, paprika, chilli powder and pepper in a bowl
4. Beat the egg in another bowl
5. Dip the pork in the egg and then coat with panko mix
6. Place in the air fryer and cook for about 12 minutes turning halfway

Chinese Chilli Beef

Servings: 2

Ingredients:

- 4 tbsp light soy sauce
- 1 tsp honey
- 3 tbsp tomato ketchup
- 1 tsp Chinese 5 spice
- 1 tbsp oil
- 6 tbsp sweet chilli sauce
- 1 tbsp lemon juice
- 400g frying steak
- 2 tbsp cornflour

Directions:

1. Slice the steak into strips, put into a bowl and cover with cornflour and 5 spice
2. Add to the air fryer and cook for 6 minutes at 200ºC
3. Whilst the beef is cooking mix together the remaining ingredients
4. Add to the air fryer and cook for another 3 minutes

Char Siu Buffalo

Servings: 2

Ingredients:

- 1 kg beef, cut into strips
- 4 tbsp honey
- 2 tbsp sugar
- 2 tbsp char siu sauce
- 2 tbsp oyster sauce
- 2 tbsp soy sauce
- 2 tbsp olive oil
- 2 tsp minced garlic
- ¼ tsp bi carbonate of soda

Directions:

1. Place all the ingredients in a bowl, mix well and marinate over night
2. Line the air fryer with foil, add the beef, keep the marinade to one side
3. Cook at 200ºC for 10 minutes
4. Brush the pork with the sauce and cook for another 20 minutes at 160ºC
5. Remove the meat and set aside
6. Strain the marinade into a saucepan, heat until it thickens
7. Drizzle over the pork and serve with rice

Simple Steaks

Servings: 2

Ingredients:

- 2 x 220-g/8-oz. sirloin steaks
- 2 teaspoons olive oil
- salt and freshly ground black pepper

Directions:

1. Bring the steaks out of the fridge an hour before cooking. Drizzle with the oil, then rub with salt and pepper on both sides. Leave to marinate at room temperature for 1 hour.
2. Preheat the air-fryer to 180°C/350°F.
3. Add the steaks to the preheated air-fryer and air-fry for 5 minutes on one side, then turn and cook for a further 4 minutes on the other side (for medium rare). Check the internal temperature of the steak has reached 58°C/135°F using a meat thermometer – if not, cook for another few minutes. Leave to rest for a few minutes before serving.

Pulled Pork, Bacon, And Cheese Sliders

Servings:2

Cooking Time:30 Minutes

Ingredients:

- 2 x 50 g / 3.5 oz pork steaks
- 1 tsp salt
- 1 tsp black pepper
- 4 slices bacon strips, chopped into small pieces
- 1 tbsp soy sauce
- 1 tbsp BBQ sauce
- 100 g / 7 oz cheddar cheese, grated
- 2 bread buns

Directions:

1. Preheat the air fryer to 200 °C / 400 °F and line the bottom of the basket with parchment paper.
2. Place the pork steaks on a clean surface and season with salt and black pepper. Move the pork steak in the prepared air fryer basket and cook for 15 minutes.
3. Remove the steak from the air fryer and shred using two forks. Mix with the chopped bacon in a heatproof bowl and place the bowl in the air fryer. Cook for 10 minutes.
4. Remove the bowl from the air fryer and stir in the soy sauce and BBQ sauce. Return the bowl to the air fryer basket and continue cooking for a further 5 minutes.
5. Meanwhile, spread the cheese across one half of the bread buns. Top with the cooked pulled pork and an extra squirt of BBQ sauce.

Kheema Meatloaf

Servings: 4

Ingredients:

- 500g minced beef
- 2 eggs
- 1 diced onion
- 200g sliced coriander
- 1 tbsp minced ginger
- ⅛ cardamom pod
- 1 tbsp minced garlic
- 2 tsp garam masala
- 1 tsp salt
- 1 tsp cayenne
- 1 tsp turmeric
- ½ tsp cinnamon

Directions:

1. Place all the ingredients in a large bowl and mix well
2. Place meat in an 8 inch pan and set air fryer to 180°C
3. Place in the air fryer and cook for 15 minutes
4. Slice and serve

Sticky Asian Beef

Servings: 2

Ingredients:

- 1 tbsp coconut oil
- 2 sliced peppers
- 25g liquid aminos
- 25g cup water
- 100g brown sugar
- ¼ tsp pepper
- ½ tsp ground ginger
- ½ tbsp minced garlic
- 1 tsp red pepper flakes
- 600g steak thinly sliced
- ¼ tsp salt

Directions:

1. Melt the coconut oil in a pan, add the peppers and cook until softened
2. In another pan add the aminos, brown sugar, ginger, garlic and pepper flakes. Mix and bring to the boil, simmer for 10 mins
3. Season the steak with salt and pepper
4. Put the steak in the air fryer and cook at 200°C for 10 minutes. Turn the steak and cook for a further 5 minutes until crispy
5. Add the steak to the peppers then mix with the sauce
6. Serve with rice

Cheesy Meatballs

Servings: 2

Ingredients:

- 500g ground beef
- 1 can of chopped green chillis
- 1 egg white
- 1 tbsp water
- 2 tbsp taco seasoning
- 16 pieces of pepper jack cheese, cut into cubes
- 300g nacho cheese tortilla chips, crushed
- 6 tbsp taco sauce
- 3 tbsp honey

Directions:

1. Take a large bowl and combine the beef with the green collie sand taco seasoning
2. Use your hands to create meatballs - you should get around 15 balls in total
3. Place a cube of cheese in the middle of each meatball, forming the ball around it once more
4. Take a small bowl and beat the egg white
5. Take a large bowl and add the crushed chips
6. Dip every meatball into the egg white and then the crushed chips
7. Place the balls into the air fryer and cook at 260°C for 14 minutes, turning halfway
8. Take a microwave-safe bowl and combine the honey and taco sauce
9. Place in the microwave for 30 seconds and serve the sauce warm with the meatballs

Lamb Calzone

Servings: 2

Ingredients:

- 1 tsp olive oil
- 1 chopped onion
- 100g baby spinach leaves
- 400g minced pork
- 250g whole wheat pizza dough
- 300g grated cheese

Directions:

1. Heat the olive oil in a pan, add the onion and cook for about 2 minutes
2. Add the spinach and cook for a further 1 ½ minutes
3. Stir in marinara sauce and the minced pork
4. Divide the dough into four and roll out into circles
5. Add ¼ of filling to each piece of dough
6. Sprinkle with cheese and fold the dough over to create half moons, crimp edges to seal
7. Spray with cooking spray, place in the air fryer and cook at 160°C for 12 minutes turning after 8 minutes

Air Fryer Roast Beef Recipe

Servings: 6
Cooking Time: 35 Mints
Ingredients:

- 900 g beef roast
- 1 tablespoon olive oil
- 1 medium onion, (optional)
- 1 teaspoon salt
- 2 teaspoons rosemary and thyme, (fresh or dried

Directions:

1. Preheat air fryer to 390°F (200°C).
2. Mix sea salt, rosemary and oil on a plate.
3. Pat the beef roast dry with paper towels. Place beef roast on plate and turn so that the oil-herb mix coats the outside of the beef.
4. If using, peel onion and cut it in half, place onion halves in the air fryer basket.
5. Place beef roast in the air fryer basket. Set to air fry beef for 5 minutes.
6. When the time is up, change the temperature to 360°F (180°C). Flip the beef roast over half way through the cooking time if required by your air fryer [Note 1].
7. Set the beef to cook for an additional 30 minutes. This should give you medium-rare beef.
8. Remove roast beef from air fryer, cover with kitchen foil and leave to rest for at least ten minutes before serving.

Honey & Mustard Meatballs

Servings: 4
Ingredients:

- 500g minced pork
- 1 red onion
- 1 tsp mustard
- 2 tsp honey
- 1 tsp garlic puree
- 1 tsp pork seasoning
- Salt and pepper

Directions:

1. Thinly slice the onion
2. Place all the ingredients in a bowl and mix until well combined
3. Form into meatballs, place in the air fryer and cook at 180ºC for 10 minutes

Steak And Mushrooms

Servings: 4

Ingredients:

- 500g cubed sirloin steak
- 300g button mushrooms
- 3 tbsp Worcestershire sauce
- 1 tbsp olive oil
- 1 tsp parsley flakes
- 1 tsp paprika
- 1 tsp crushed chilli flakes

Directions:

1. Combine all ingredients in a bowl, cover and chill for at least 4 hours
2. Preheat air fryer to 200ºC
3. Drain and discard the marinade from the steak
4. Place the steak and mushrooms in the air fryer and cook for 5 minutes
5. Toss and cook for a further 5 minutes

Beef Stuffed Peppers

Servings: 4

Ingredients:

- 4 bell peppers
- ½ chopped onion
- 1 minced garlic clove
- 500g minced beef
- 5 tbsp tomato sauce
- 100g grated cheese
- 2 tsp Worcestershire sauce
- 1 tsp garlic powder
- A pinch of black pepper
- ½ tsp chilli powder
- 1 tsp dried basil
- 75g cooked rice

Directions:

1. Cook the onions, minced beef, garlic and all the seasonings until the meat is browned
2. Remove from the heat and add Worcestershire sauce, rice, ½ the cheese and ⅔ of the tomato sauce mix well
3. Cut the tops off the peppers and remove the seeds
4. Stuff the peppers with the mixture and place in the air fryer
5. Cook at 200ºC for about 11 minutes
6. When there are 3 minutes remaining top the peppers with the rest of the tomato sauce and cheese

Traditional Pork Chops

Servings: 8

Ingredients:

- 8 pork chops
- 1 egg
- 100ml milk
- 300g bread crumbs
- 1 packet of dry ranch seasoning mix
- Salt and pepper to taste

Directions:

1. Preheat air fryer to 170ºC
2. Beat the egg in a bowl, add the milk season with salt and pepper
3. In another bowl mix the bread crumbs and ranch dressing mix
4. Dip the pork into the egg then cover with breadcrumbs
5. Place in the air fryer and cook for 12 minutes turning half way

Pork Schnitzel

Servings: 2

Ingredients:

- 3 pork steaks, cut into cubes
- Salt and pepper
- 175g flour
- 2 eggs
- 175g breadcrumbs

Directions:

1. Sprinkle the pork with salt and pepper
2. Coat in the flour then dip in the egg
3. Coat the pork in breadcrumbs
4. Place in the air fryer and cook at 175ºC for 20 minutes turning halfway
5. Serve with red cabbage

Mini Moroccan Lamb Burgers

Servings: 2

Ingredients:

- 400 g/14 oz. minced/ground lamb
- 1 tablespoon freshly chopped coriander/cilantro
- 1 teaspoon freshly chopped mint
- ½ teaspoon smoked paprika
- 1 teaspoon ground cumin
- 1 tablespoon harissa paste
- tzatziki , to serve
- pitta breads and salad leaves, to serve

Directions:

1. Combine all the ingredients in a food processor, then divide into 6 equal portions and mould into burgers.
2. Preheat the air-fryer to 180°C/350°F.
3. Add the burgers to the preheated air-fryer and air-fry for 9 minutes, turning halfway through cooking. Check the internal temperature of the burgers has reached at least 75°C/170°F using a meat thermometer – if not, cook for another few minutes. Serve tucked into warmed pitta breads, with salad leaves and tzatziki.

Air Fryer Pork Bratwurst

Servings: 2

Ingredients:

- 2 pork bratwursts
- 2 hotdog bread rolls
- 2 tbsp tomato sauce

Directions:

1. Preheat the air fryer to 200°C
2. Place the bratwurst in the fryer and cook for 10 minutes, turning halfway
3. Remove and place in the open bread rolls
4. Place back into the air fryer for 1 to 2 minutes, until the read is slightly crisped
5. Enjoy with the tomato sauce either on top or on the side

Sausage Gnocchi One Pot

Servings: 2

Ingredients:

- 4 links of sausage
- 250g green beans, washed and cut into halves
- 1 tsp Italian seasoning
- 1 tbsp olive oil
- 300g gnocchi
- Salt and pepper for seasoning

Directions:

1. Preheat the air fryer to 220°C
2. Cut the sausage up into pieces
3. Take a bowl and add the gnocchi and green beans, along with the oil and season
4. Place the sausage into the fryer first and then the rest of the ingredients
5. Cook for 12 minutes, giving everything a stir halfway through

Breaded Bone-in Pork Chops

Servings: 2

Ingredients:

- 2 pork chops with the bone in
- 250g Italian breadcrumbs
- 2 tbsp mayonnaise
- 1/2 tsp garlic powder
- 1/2 tsp onion powder
- 1/2 tsp thyme
- 1/2 tsp paprika
- Salt and pepper to taste

Directions:

1. Preheat the air fryer to 260°C
2. Take a large bowl and add the breadcrumbs, garlic powder, paprika, salt and pepper, and thyme, and onion powder, combining well
3. Cover the pork chops with the mayonnaise making sure to cover both sides
4. Coat the meat with the seasoning mixture, making sure it is fully covered
5. Cook the pork chops in the fryer for 10 minutes, turning over halfway

Fish & Seafood Recipes

Maine Seafood

Servings: 2

Ingredients:

- 500g flour
- 400g breadcrumbs
- 300g steamer clams
- 3 eggs
- 3 tbsp water

Directions:

1. Soak the clams for 3 hours, drain and rinse
2. Bring 1 inch of water to boil, add the clams and cover with a lid, steam for about 7 minutes until the clams open.
3. Remove the clams from the shell and set aside
4. Put the eggs in a bowl and mix with the water
5. Dip the clams in the flour, then the egg and then coat in breadcrumbs
6. Heat the air fryer to 180°C and cook for about 7 minutes

Air Fried Shrimp Manchurian

Servings: 4

Cooking Time: 20 Mints

Ingredients:

- 400 g Popcorn shrimp
- 3 garlic pods (minced)
- ½ inch ginger (grated)
- ½ of a medium-sized onion (cubed)
- 1 tbsp soya sauce 1 tsp chili garlic sauce
- 1 tbsp green chili sauce
- 1 tbsp tomato ketchup
- ½ tsp black pepper
- Corn flour slurry: 1 tbsp corn flour + 2 tbsp water (mixed)
- 2 spring onions (chopped)
- Oil (as required)

Directions:

1. Cook the half of the bag of the Popcorn Shrimp in your air fryer at 200°C/400°F for 8 – 10 minutes, until reaching an internal temperature of 165°C/320°F or higher.

2. Prepare the sauce by whisking soya sauce, chili garlic sauce, green chili sauce, tomato ketchup and black pepper in a bowl.

3. Heat oil in a pan, sauté ginger and garlic. Add the onions and sauté for 2 mins. Follow by adding the prepared sauce, corn flour slurry, and mix everything together.

4. Add the air fried Popcorn Shrimp, toss everything together to combine. Garnish with spring onions.

5. Serve hot! This dish goes well as a side with fried rice, white rice, or with hakka noodles, or is good as an appetizer on its own.

Thai Fish Cakes

Servings: 4

Ingredients:

- 200g pre-mashed potatoes
- 2 fillets of white fish, flaked and mashed
- 1 onion
- 1 tsp butter
- 1 tsp milk
- 1 lime zest and rind
- 3 tsp chilli
- 1 tsp Worcester sauce
- 1 tsp coriander
- 1 tsp mixed spice
- 1 tsp mixed herbs
- 50g breadcrumbs
- Salt and pepper to taste

Directions:

1. Cover the white fish in milk
2. in a mixing bowl place the fish and add the seasoning and mashed potatoes
3. Add the butter and remaining milk
4. Use your hands to create patties and place in the refrigerator for 3 hours
5. Preheat your air fryer to 200ºC
6. Cook for 15 minutes

Cajun Shrimp Boil

Servings: 6

Ingredients:

- 300g cooked shrimp
- 14 slices of smoked sausage
- 5 par boiled potatoes, cut into halves
- 4 mini corn on the cobs, quartered
- 1 diced onion
- 3 tbsp old bay seasoning
- Olive oil spray

Directions:

1. Combine all the ingredients in a bowl and mix well
2. Line the air fryer with foil
3. Place half the mix into the air fryer and cook at 200ºC for about 6 minutes, mix the ingredients and cook for a further 6 minutes.
4. Repeat for the second batch

Air Fryer Spicy Bay Scallops

Servings: 4
Cooking Time: 10 Mints
Ingredients:

- 454 g bay scallops, rinsed and patted dry
- 2 teaspoons smoked paprika
- 2 teaspoons chili powder
- 2 teaspoons olive oil
- 1 teaspoon garlic powder
- ¼ teaspoon ground black pepper
- ⅛ teaspoon cayenne red pepper

Directions:

1. Preheat an air fryer to 400°F/200°C.
2. Combine bay scallops, smoked paprika, chili powder, olive oil, garlic powder, pepper, and cayenne pepper in a bowl; stir until evenly combined. Transfer to the air fryer basket.
3. Air fry until scallops are cooked through, about 8 minutes, shaking basket halfway through the cooking time.

Panko-crusted Air Fryer Mahi Mahi

Servings: 4
Cooking Time: 15 Mints
Ingredients:

- 4 (4 ounce) mahi mahi fillets
- 2 tablespoons grapeseed oil
- 2 cups panko bread crumbs
- 1 teaspoon of everything bagel seasoning
- ½ teaspoon garlic salt
- ½ teaspoon ground turmeric
- ½ teaspoon ground black pepper
- nonstick cooking spray
- 1 teaspoon chopped fresh parsley
- 1 medium lemon, cut into 4 wedges

Directions:

1. Preheat an air fryer to 400°F/200°C for 5 minutes.
2. Meanwhile, place mahi mahi fillets on a platter and drizzle with grapeseed oil.
3. Mix panko, bagel seasoning, garlic salt, turmeric, and pepper together in a shallow dish. Dip each fillet into the panko mixture to coat, then place in a single layer in the air fryer basket. Spray with nonstick spray.
4. Cook in the preheated air fryer until fish flakes easily with a fork, 12 to 15 minutes, flipping halfway through.
5. Remove from the air fryer. Garnish with parsley and lemon wedges. Serve immediately.

Salmon Patties

Servings: 4

Ingredients:

- 400g salmon
- 1 egg
- 1 diced onion
- 200g breadcrumbs
- 1 tsp dill weed

Directions:

1. Remove all bones and skin from the salmon
2. Mix egg, onion, dill weed and bread crumbs with the salmon
3. Shape mixture into patties and place into the air fryer
4. Set air fryer to 180°C
5. Cook for 5 minutes then turn them over and cook for a further 5 minutes until golden brown

Extra Crispy Popcorn Shrimp

Servings: 2

Ingredients:

- 300g Frozen popcorn shrimp
- 1 tsp cayenne pepper
- Salt and pepper for seasoning

Directions:

1. Preheat the air fryer to 220°C
2. Place the shrimp inside the air fryer and cook for 6 minutes, giving them a shake at the halfway point
3. Remove and season with salt and pepper, and the cayenne to your liking

Shrimp With Yum Yum Sauce

Servings: 4

Ingredients:

- 400g peeled jumbo shrimp
- 1 tbsp soy sauce
- 1 tbsp garlic paste
- 1 tbsp ginger paste
- 4 tbsp mayo
- 2 tbsp ketchup
- 1 tbsp sugar
- 1 tsp paprika
- 1 tsp garlic powder

Directions:

1. Mix soy sauce, garlic paste and ginger paste in a bowl. Add the shrimp, allow to marinate for 15 minutes
2. In another bowl mix ketchup, mayo, sugar, paprika and the garlic powder to make the yum yum sauce.
3. Set the air fryer to 200ºC, place shrimp in the basket and cook for 8-10 minutes

Air Fryer Shake N Bake Style Fish

Servings: 4

Cooking Time: 10 Mints

Ingredients:

- 454 g white fish fillets (cod, halibut, tilapia, etc.)
- 125 g Ice water, beaten egg, milk, or mayo , to moisten the fish

Directions:

1. Preheat Air Fryer at 380°F/195°C for 4 minutes.
2. Cut fish fillets in half if needed. Make sure they are even sized so they'll cook evenly. Moisten the fish based on seasoned coating instructions . Coat with the seasoned coating mix.
3. Spray an air fryer basket/tray with oil or place a perforated parchment sheet in the air fryer basket/tray & lightly coat with oil spray
4. Place the coated fish in a single layer. Make sure the fish is not touching or the coating may flake off when you flip them. Lightly coat with oil spray.
5. Air Fry at 380°F/193°C for 8-14 minutes, depending on the size and thickness of your fillets. After 6 minutes, flip the filets. Lightly spray any dry spots than then continue cooking for the remaining time or until they are crispy brown and the fish is cooked through. Serve with your favorite dip: tartar sauce, mustard, aioli, etc.

Cajun Prawn Skewers

Servings: 2

Ingredients:

- 350 g/12 oz. king prawns/jumbo shrimp
- MARINADE
- 1 teaspoon smoked paprika
- 1 teaspoon unrefined sugar
- 1 teaspoon salt
- ½ teaspoon onion powder
- ½ teaspoon mustard powder
- ¼ teaspoon dried oregano
- ¼ teaspoon dried thyme
- 1 teaspoon white wine vinegar
- 2 teaspoons olive oil

Directions:

1. Mix all the marinade ingredients together in a bowl. Mix the prawns/shrimp into the marinade and cover. Place in the fridge to marinate for at least an hour.
2. Preheat the air-fryer to 180ºC/350ºF.
3. Thread 4–5 prawns/shrimp on to each skewer (you should have enough for 4–5 skewers). Add the skewers to the preheated air-fryer and air-fry for 2 minutes, then turn the skewers and cook for a further 2 minutes. Check the internal temperature of the prawns/shrimp has reached at least 50ºC/125ºF using a meat thermometer – if not, cook for another few minutes. Serve immediately.

Pesto Salmon

Servings: 4

Ingredients:

- 4 x 150–175-g/5½–6-oz. salmon fillets
- lemon wedges, to serve
- PESTO
- 50 g/scant ½ cup toasted pine nuts
- 50 g/2 oz. fresh basil
- 50 g/⅔ cup grated Parmesan or Pecorino
- 100 ml/7 tablespoons olive oil

Directions:

1. To make the pesto, blitz the pine nuts, basil and Parmesan to a paste in a food processor. Pour in the olive oil and process again.
2. Preheat the air-fryer to 160ºC/325ºF.
3. Top each salmon fillet with 2 tablespoons of the pesto. Add the salmon fillets to the preheated air-fryer and air-fry for 9 minutes. Check the internal temperature of the fish has reached at least 63ºC/145ºF using a meat thermometer – if not, cook for another few minutes.

Crunchy Fish

Servings: 4

Ingredients:

- 200g dry breadcrumbs
- 4 tbsp olive oil
- 4 fillets of white fish
- 1 beaten egg
- 1 sliced lemon

Directions:

1. Heat the fryer to 180°C
2. In a medium mixing bowl, combine the olive oil and the breadcrumbs
3. Take the fish and first dip it into the egg and then the breadcrumbs, making sure they are evenly coated well
4. Arrange the fish into the basket
5. Cook for 12 minutes
6. Remove and serve with lemon slices

Air Fryer Healthy White Fish With Garlic & Lemon

Servings: 2

Cooking Time: 10 Mints

Ingredients:

- 340 g tilapia filets , or other white fish (2 filets-6 ounces each)
- 1/2 teaspoon garlic powder
- 1/2 teaspoon lemon pepper seasoning
- 1/2 teaspoon onion powder , optional
- kosher salt or sea salt , to taste
- fresh cracked black pepper , to taste
- fresh chopped parsley
- lemon wedges

Directions:

1. Pre-heat Air Fryer to 360°F/180°C for 5 minutes. Rinse and pat dry the fish filets. Spray or coat with olive oil spray and season with garlic powder, lemon pepper, and/or onion power, salt and pepper. Repeat for both sides.

2. To help sticking, lay perforated air fryer baking paper inside base of air fryer. Lightly spray the paper. (if not using a liner, spray enough olive oil spray at the base of the air fryer basket to make sure fish does not stick)

3. Lay the fish on top of the paper. Add a few lemon wedges next to fish.Air Fry at 360°F/180°C for about 6-12 minutes, or until fish can be flaked with a fork. Timing will depend on the thickness of the filets, how cold the filets are, & individual preference

Air Fried Popcorn Shrimp With Mango And Avocado Salad

Servings: 4
Cooking Time: 10 Mints
Ingredients:
- 1/2 lemon, juice and finely grated zest
- 2 tablespoons extra virgin olive oil
- 1 teaspoon honey
- 1/4 teaspoon salt fresh ground pepper to taste
- For the salad:
- 1 package Gorton's Popcorn Shrimp
- 100 g/4 cups mixed greens
- 1 mango, diced
- 1 avocado, diced
- 1 small cucumber, sliced

Directions:
1. Cook the half of the bag of the Popcorn Shrimp in your air fryer at 200°C/400°F for 8 – 10 minutes, until reaching an internal temperature of 165°C/320°F or higher.
2. In a small bowl, add the dressing ingredients and mix well.
3. In a large bowl, combine the greens, mango, avocado and cucumber.
4. Top with the shrimp when ready and drizzle with the dressing. Enjoy!

Peppery Lemon Shrimp

Servings: 2
Ingredients:
- 300g uncooked shrimp
- 1 tbsp olive oil
- 1 the juice of 1 lemon
- 0.25 tsp garlic powder
- 1 sliced lemon
- 1 tsp pepper
- 0.25 tsp paprika

Directions:
1. Heat the fryer to 200ºC
2. Take a medium sized mixing bowl and combine the lemon juice, pepper, garlic powder, paprika and the olive oil together
3. Add the shrimp to the bowl and make sure they're well coated
4. Arrange the shrimp into the basket of the fryer
5. Cook for between 6-8 minutes, until firm and pink

Baked Panko Cod

Servings: 5

Ingredients:

- 400g cod, cut into 5 pieces
- 250g panko breadcrumbs
- 1 egg plus 1 egg white extra
- Cooking spray
- ½ tsp onion powder
- ½ tsp garlic salt
- ⅛ tsp black pepper
- ½ tsp mixed herbs

Directions:

1. Heat air fryer to 220ºC
2. Beat the egg and egg white in a bowl
3. Sprinkle fish with herbs and spice mix, dip into the egg and then cover in the panko bread crumbs
4. Line air fryer basket with tin foil. Place the fish in the air fryer and coat with cooking spray
5. Cook for about 15 minutes until, fish is lightly browned

Air Fryer Tuna

Servings: 2

Ingredients:

- 2 tuna steaks, boneless and skinless
- 2 tsp honey
- 1 tsp grated ginger
- 4 tbsp soy sauce
- 1 tsp sesame oil
- 1/2 tsp rice vinegar

Directions:

1. Combine the honey, soy sauce, rice vinegar and sesame oil in a bowl until totally mixed together
2. Cover the tuna steaks with the sauce and place in the refrigerator for half an hour to marinade
3. Preheat the air fryer to 270ºC
4. Cook the tuna for 4 minutes
5. Allow to rest before slicing

Air Fried Scallops

Servings: 2

Ingredients:

- 6 scallops
- 1 tbsp olive oil
- Salt and pepper to taste

Directions:

1. Brush the filets with olive oil
2. Sprinkle with salt and pepper
3. Place in the air fryer and cook at 200ºC for 2 mins
4. Turn the scallops over and cook for another 2 minutes

Air Fried Shrimp Sub

Servings: 4

Cooking Time: 10 Mints

Ingredients:

- French rolls
- Remolade Sauce (found in the dressing aisle at any grocery store)
- Shredded lettuce
- Sliced tomatoes
- Gorton's Popcorn Shrimp

Directions:

1. Set your air fryer to 200°C/400° and toss in half the bag of your frozen popcorn shrimp. Cook for about 8 – 10 minutes, until reaching an internal temperature of 165°C/320°F or higher.
2. In the meantime, lather remoulade sauce on your French roll.
3. Once the shrimp is crispy, build your po' boy with lettuce and tomatoes. Enjoy!

Air Fried Shrimp Po Boy

Servings: 6
Cooking Time: 5 Mints
Ingredients:

- 1 box of Popcorn Shrim
- 6 French Rolls or Brioche Hot Dog buns
- 57 g/4 tbsp unsalted butter
- 150 g/2 cups shredded lettuce
- 2 large tomatoes, sliced
- For the remoulade sauce:
- 230 g/1 cup mayonnaise
- 2 tbsp dijon mustard
- 1 tsp smoked paprika
- 1 tsp old bay seasoning
- 1 tsp horseradish
- 2 tbsp dill pickle relish
- 2 cloves garlic, minced
- 1 tsp hot sauce
- 2 green onions, finely chopped
- 2 tbsp lemon juice
- 1 tsp Worcestershire sauce
- 1/4 tsp sea salt
- 1/4 tsp ground black pepper

Directions:

1. Combine all ingredients for remoulade sauce and set on the side.
2. Cook half of the bag of the Popcorn Shrimp in your air fryer at 200°C/400°F for 8 – 10 minutes, until reaching an internal temperature of 165°C/320°F or higher.
3. Spread butter on french rolls and toast for 2-3 minutes.
4. Fill french rolls with lettuce, tomatoes, Popcorn Shrimp, and drizzled remoulade sauce. Serve and enjoy!

Coconut Shrimp

Servings: 4

Ingredients:

- 250g flour
- 1 ½ tsp black pepper
- 2 eggs
- 150g unsweetened flaked coconut
- 1 Serrano chilli, thinly sliced
- 25g panko bread crumbs
- 300g shrimp raw
- ½ tsp salt
- 4 tbsp honey
- 25ml lime juice

Directions:

1. Mix together flour and pepper, in another bowl beat the eggs and in another bowl mix the panko and coconut
2. Dip each of the shrimp in the flour mix then the egg and then cover in the coconut mix
3. Coat the shrimp in cooking spray
4. Place in the air fryer and cook at 200ºC for 6-8 mins turning half way through
5. Mix together the honey, lime juice and chilli and serve with the shrimp

Side Dishes Recipes
Corn On The Cob

Servings: 4

Ingredients:

- 75g mayo
- 2 tsp grated cheese
- 1 tsp lime juice
- ¼ tsp chilli powder
- 2 ears of corn, cut into 4

Directions:

1. Heat the air fryer to 200ºC
2. Mix the mayo, cheese lime juice and chilli powder in a bowl
3. Cover the corn in the mayo mix
4. Place in the air fryer and cook for 8 minutes

Sweet Potato Wedges

Servings:4
Cooking Time:20 Minutes
Ingredients:

- ½ tsp garlic powder
- ½ tsp cumin
- ½ tsp smoked paprika
- ½ tsp cayenne pepper
- ½ tsp salt
- ½ tsp black pepper
- 1 tsp dried chives
- 4 tbsp olive oil
- 3 large sweet potatoes, cut into wedges

Directions:

1. Preheat the air fryer to 180 °C / 350 °F and line the bottom of the basket with parchment paper.
2. In a bowl, mix the garlic powder, cumin, smoked paprika, cayenne pepper, salt, black pepper, and dried chives until combined.
3. Whisk in the olive oil and coat the sweet potato wedges in the spicy oil mixture.
4. Transfer the coated sweet potatoes to the air fryer and close the lid. Cook for 20 minutes until cooked and crispy. Serve hot as a side with your main meal.

Asparagus Fries

Servings: 2
Ingredients:

- 1 egg
- 1 tsp honey
- 100g panko bread crumbs
- Pinch of cayenne pepper
- 100g grated parmesan
- 12 asparagus spears
- 75g mustard
- 75g Greek yogurt

Directions:

1. Preheat air fryer to 200ºC
2. Combine egg and honey in a bowl, mix panko crumbs and parmesan on a plate
3. Coat each asparagus in egg then in the bread crumbs
4. Place in the air fryer and cook for about 6 mins
5. Mix the remaining ingredients in a bowl and serve as a dipping sauce

Homemade Croquettes

Servings:4
Cooking Time:15 Minutes
Ingredients:

- 400 g / 14 oz white rice, uncooked
- 1 onion, sliced
- 2 cloves garlic, finely sliced
- 2 eggs, beaten
- 50 g / 3.5 oz parmesan cheese, grated
- 1 tsp salt
- 1 tsp black pepper
- 50 g / 3.5 oz breadcrumbs
- 1 tsp dried oregano

Directions:

1. In a large mixing bowl, combine the white rice, onion slices, garlic cloves slices, one beaten egg, parmesan cheese, and a sprinkle of salt and pepper.
2. Whisk the second egg in a separate bowl and place the breadcrumbs into another bowl.
3. Shape the mixture into 12 even croquettes and roll evenly in the egg, followed by the breadcrumbs.
4. Preheat the air fryer to 190 °C / 375 °F and line the bottom of the basket with parchment paper.
5. Place the croquettes in the lined air fryer basket and cook for 15 minutes, turning halfway through, until crispy and golden. Enjoy while hot as a side to your main dish.

Courgette Chips

Servings: 4
Ingredients:

- 250g panko bread crumbs
- 100g grated parmesan
- 1 medium courgette, thinly sliced
- 1 egg beaten

Directions:

1. Preheat the air fryer to 175ºC
2. Combine the breadcrumbs and parmesan
3. Dip the courgette into the egg then coat in bread crumbs
4. Spray with cooking spray and cook in the air fryer for 10 minutes
5. Turnover with tongs and cook for a further 2 minutes

Potato Wedges

Servings: 4

Ingredients:

- 2 potatoes, cut into wedges
- 1 ½ tbsp olive oil
- ½ tsp paprika
- ⅛ tsp ground black pepper
- ½ tsp parsley flakes
- ½ tsp chilli powder
- ½ tsp sea salt

Directions:

1. Preheat the air fryer to 200°C
2. Add all ingredients to a bowl and combine well
3. Place the wedges into the air fryer and cook for 10 minutes
4. Turn and cook for a further 8 minutes until golden brown

Super Easy Fries

Servings: 2

Ingredients:

- 500g potatoes cut into ½ inch sticks
- 1 tsp olive oil
- ¼ tsp salt
- ¼ tsp pepper

Directions:

1. Place the potatoes in a bowl cover with water and allow to soak for 30 minutes
2. Spread the butter onto one side of the bread slices
3. Pat dry with paper, drizzle with oil and toss to coat
4. Place in the air fryer and cook at 200°C for about 15 minutes, keep tossing through cooking time
5. Sprinkle with salt and pepper

Cheesy Garlic Asparagus

Servings: 4

Ingredients:

- 1 tsp olive oil
- 500g asparagus
- 1 tsp garlic salt
- 1 tbsp grated parmesan cheese
- Salt and pepper for seasoning

Directions:

1. Preheat the air fryer to 270°C
2. Clean the asparagus and cut off the bottom 1"
3. Pat dry and place in the air fryer, covering with the oil
4. Sprinkle the parmesan and garlic salt on top, seasoning to your liking
5. Cook for between 7 and 10 minutes
6. Add a little extra parmesan over the top before serving

Bbq Beetroot Crisps

Servings:4

Cooking Time:5 Minutes

Ingredients:

- 400 g / 14 oz beetroot, sliced
- 2 tbsp olive oil
- 1 tbsp BBQ seasoning
- ½ tsp black pepper

Directions:

1. Preheat the air fryer to 180 °C / 350 °F and line the bottom of the basket with parchment paper.
2. Place the beetroot slices in a large bowl. Add the olive oil, BBQ seasoning, and black pepper, and toss to coat the beetroot slices on both sides.
3. Place the beetroot slices in the air fryer and cook for 5 minutes until hot and crispy.

Sweet And Sticky Parsnips And Carrots

Servings:2

Cooking Time:15 Minutes

Ingredients:

- 4 large carrots, peeled and chopped into long chunks
- 4 large parsnips, peeled and chopped into long chunks
- 1 tbsp olive oil
- 2 tbsp honey
- 1 tsp dried mixed herbs

Directions:

1. Preheat the air fryer to 150 °C / 300 °F and line the bottom of the basket with parchment paper.
2. Place the chopped carrots and parsnips in a large bowl and drizzle over the olive oil and honey. Sprinkle in some black pepper to taste and toss well to fully coat the vegetables.
3. Transfer the coated vegetables into the air fryer basket and shut the lid. Cook for 20 minutes until the carrots and parsnips and cooked and crispy.
4. Serve as a side with your dinner.

Shishito Peppers

Servings: 2

Ingredients:

- 200g shishito peppers
- Salt and pepper to taste
- ½ tbsp avocado oil
- 75g grated cheese
- 2 limes

Directions:

1. Rinse the peppers
2. Place in a bowl and mix with oil, salt and pepper
3. Place in the air fryer and cook at 175ºC for 10 minutes
4. Place on a serving plate and sprinkle with cheese

Potato Wedges With Rosemary

Servings: 2

Ingredients:

- 2 potatoes, sliced into wedges
- 1 tbsp olive oil
- 2 tsp seasoned salt
- 2 tbsp chopped rosemary

Directions:

1. Preheat air fryer to 190°C
2. Drizzle potatoes with oil, mix in salt and rosemary
3. Place in the air fryer and cook for 20 minutes turning halfway

Air Fryer Eggy Bread

Servings:2

Cooking Time:5-7 Minutes

Ingredients:

- 4 slices white bread
- 4 eggs, beaten
- 1 tsp black pepper
- 1 tsp dried chives

Directions:

1. Preheat your air fryer to 150 °C / 300 °F and line the bottom of the basket with parchment paper.
2. Whisk the eggs in a large mixing bowl and soak each slice of bread until fully coated.
3. Transfer the eggy bread to the preheated air fryer and cook for 5-7 minutes until the eggs are set and the bread is crispy.
4. Serve hot with a sprinkle of black pepper and chives on top.

Ricotta Stuffed Aubergine

Servings: 2

Ingredients:

- 1 aubergine
- 150g ricotta cheese
- 75g Parmesan cheese, plus an extra 75g for the breading
- 1 tsp garlic powder
- 3 tbsp parsley
- 1 egg, plus an extra 2 eggs for the breading
- 300g pork rind crumbs
- 2 tsp Italian seasoning

Directions:

1. Cut the aubergine into rounds, about 1/2" in thickness
2. Line a baking sheet with parchment and arrange the rounds on top, sprinkling with salt
3. Place another sheet of parchment on top and place something heavy on top to get rid of excess water
4. Leave for 30 minutes
5. Take a bowl and combine the egg, ricotta, 75g Parmesan and parsley, until smooth
6. Remove the parchment from the aubergine and wipe off the salt
7. Take a tablespoon of the ricotta mixture and place on top of each round of aubergine, spreading with a knife
8. Place in the freezer for a while to set
9. Take a bowl and add the two eggs, the pork rinds, parmesan and seasonings, and combine
10. Remove the aubergine from the freezer and coat each one in the mixture completely
11. Place back in the freezer for 45 minutes
12. Cook in the air fryer for 8 minutes at 250°C

Crispy Cinnamon French Toast

Servings:2
Cooking Time:5 Minutes
Ingredients:

- 4 slices white bread
- 4 eggs
- 200 ml milk (cow's milk, cashew milk, soy milk, or oat milk)
- 2 tbsp granulated sugar
- 1 tsp brown sugar
- 1 tsp vanilla extract
- ½ tsp ground cinnamon

Directions:

1. Preheat your air fryer to 150 °C / 300 °F and line the bottom of the basket with parchment paper.
2. Cut each of the bread slices into 2 even rectangles and set them aside.
3. In a mixing bowl, whisk together the 4 eggs, milk, granulated sugar, brown sugar, vanilla extract, and ground cinnamon.
4. Soak the bread pieces in the egg mixture until they are fully covered and soaked in the mixture.
5. Place the coated bread slices in the lined air fryer, close the lid, and cook for 4-5 minutes until the bread is crispy and golden.
6. Serve the French toast slices with whatever toppings you desire.

Mexican Rice

Servings: 4

Ingredients:

- 500g long grain rice
- 3 tbsp olive oil
- 60ml water
- 1 tsp chilli powder
- 1/4 tsp cumin
- 2 tbsp tomato paste
- 1/2 tsp garlic powder
- 1tsp red pepper flakes
- 1 chopped onion
- 500ml chicken stock
- Half a small jalapeño pepper with seeds out, chopped
- Salt for seasoning

Directions:

1. Add the water and tomato paste and combine, placing to one side
2. Take a baking pan and add a little oil
3. Wash the rice and add to the baking pan
4. Add the chicken stock, tomato paste, jalapeños, onions, and the rest of the olive oil, and combine
5. Place aluminium foil over the top and place in your air fryer
6. Cook at 220ºC for 50 minutes
7. Keep checking the rice as it cooks, as the liquid should be absorbing

Cauliflower With Hot Sauce And Blue Cheese Sauce

Servings:2
Cooking Time:15 Minutes
Ingredients:

- For the cauliflower:
- 1 cauliflower, broken into florets
- 4 tbsp hot sauce
- 2 tbsp olive oil
- 1 tsp garlic powder
- ½ tsp salt
- ½ tsp black pepper
- 1 tbsp plain flour
- 1 tbsp corn starch
- For the blue cheese sauce:
- 50 g / 1.8 oz blue cheese, crumbled
- 2 tbsp sour cream
- 2 tbsp mayonnaise
- ½ tsp salt
- ½ tsp black pepper

Directions:

1. Preheat the air fryer to 180 °C / 350 °F and line the bottom of the basket with parchment paper.
2. In a bowl, combine the hot sauce, olive oil, garlic powder, salt, and black pepper until it forms a consistent mixture. Add the cauliflower to the bowl and coat in the sauce.
3. Stir in the plain flour and corn starch until well combined.
4. Transfer the cauliflower to the lined basket in the air fryer, close the lid, and cook for 12-15 minutes until the cauliflower has softened and is golden in colour.
5. Meanwhile, make the blue cheese sauce by combining all of the ingredients. When the cauliflower is ready, remove it from the air fryer and serve with the blue cheese sauce on the side.

Celery Root Fries

Servings: 2

Ingredients:

- ½ celeriac, cut into sticks
- 500ml water
- 1 tbsp lime juice
- 1 tbsp olive oil
- 75g mayo
- 1 tbsp mustard
- 1 tbsp powdered horseradish

Directions:

1. Put celeriac in a bowl, add water and lime juice, soak for 30 minutes
2. Preheat air fryer to 200
3. Mix together the mayo, horseradish powder and mustard, refrigerate
4. Drain the celeriac, drizzle with oil and season with salt and pepper
5. Place in the air fryer and cook for about 10 minutes turning halfway
6. Serve with the mayo mix as a dip

Vegetarian & Vegan Recipes
Roasted Garlic

Servings: 2

Ingredients:

- 1 head of garlic
- Drizzle of olive oil
- Salt and pepper for seasoning

Directions:

1. Remove paper peel from garlic
2. Place in foil and drizzle with oil
3. Place in the air fryer and cook at 200ºC for 20 minutes
4. Season before serving

Bagel Pizza

Servings: 1

Ingredients:

- 1 bagel
- 2 tbsp marinara sauce
- 6 slices vegan pepperoni
- 2 tbsp mozzarella
- Pinch of basil

Directions:

1. Heat the air fryer to 180ºC
2. Cut the bagel in half and toast for 2 minutes in the air fryer
3. Remove from the air fryer and top with marinara sauce, pepperoni and mozzarella
4. Return to the air fryer and cook for 4-5 minutes
5. Sprinkle with basil to serve

Crispy Broccoli

Servings: 2

Ingredients:

- 170 g/6 oz. broccoli florets
- 2 tablespoons olive oil
- ⅛ teaspoon garlic salt
- ⅛ teaspoon freshly ground black pepper
- 2 tablespoons freshly grated Parmesan or Pecorino

Directions:

1. Preheat the air-fryer to 200ºC/400ºF.
2. Toss the broccoli in the oil, season with the garlic salt and pepper, then toss over the grated cheese and combine well. Add the broccoli to the preheated air-fryer and air-fry for 5 minutes, giving the broccoli a stir halfway through to ensure even cooking.

Butternut Squash

Servings: 4

Ingredients:

- 500 g/1 lb. 2 oz. butternut squash, chopped into 2.5-cm/1-in. cubes
- 1 tablespoon olive oil or avocado oil
- 1 teaspoon smoked paprika
- 1 teaspoon dried oregano
- ½ teaspoon salt
- ¼ teaspoon freshly ground black pepper

Directions:

1. Preheat the air-fryer to 180°C/350°F.
2. In a bowl toss the butternut squash cubes in the oil and all the seasonings.
3. Add the butternut squash cubes to the preheated air-fryer and air-fry for 16–18 minutes, shaking the drawer once during cooking.

Honey Roasted Parsnips

Servings: 4

Ingredients:

- 350 g/12 oz. parsnips
- 1 tablespoon plain/all-purpose flour (gluten-free if you wish)
- 1½ tablespoons runny honey
- 2 tablespoons olive oil
- salt

Directions:

1. Top and tail the parsnips, then slice lengthways, about 2 cm/¾ in. wide. Place in a saucepan with water to cover and a good pinch of salt. Bring to the boil, then boil for 5 minutes.
2. Remove and drain well, allowing any excess water to evaporate. Dust the parsnips with flour. Mix together the honey and oil in a small bowl, then toss in the parsnips to coat well in the honey and oil.
3. Preheat the air-fryer to 180°C/350°F.
4. Add the parsnips to the preheated air-fryer and air-fry for 14–16 minutes, depending on how dark you like the outsides (the longer you cook them, the sweeter they get).

Bbq Soy Curls

Servings: 2

Ingredients:

- 250ml warm water
- 1 tsp vegetable bouillon
- 200g soy curls
- 40g BBQ sauce
- 1 tsp oil

Directions:

1. Soak the soy curls in water and bouillon for 10 minutes
2. Place the soy curls in another bowl and shred
3. Heat the air fryer to 200°C
4. Cook for 3 minutes
5. Remove from the air fryer and coat in bbq sauce
6. Return to the air fryer and cook for 5 minutes shaking halfway through

Air Fryer Crispy Potatoes

Servings: 4

Cooking Time: 5 Mints

Ingredients:

- 450 g baby potatoes, halved
- 1 tbsp. extra-virgin olive oil
- 1 tsp. garlic powder
- 1 tsp. Italian seasoning
- 1 tsp. Cajun seasoning (optional)
- Salt
- Freshlyground black pepper
- Lemon wedge, for serving
- Freshly chopped parsley, for garnish

Directions:

1. In a large bowl, toss potatoes with oil, garlic powder, Italian seasoning, and Cajun seasoning, if using. Season with salt and pepper.

2. Place potatoes in basket of air fryer and cook at 200°C/400°F for 10 minutes. Shake basket and stir potatoes and cook until potatoes are golden and tender, 8 to 10 minutes more.

3. Squeeze lemon juice over cooked potatoes and garnish with parsley before serving

Roasted Cauliflower

Servings: 2

Ingredients:

- 3 cloves garlic
- 1 tbsp peanut oil
- ½ tsp salt
- ½ tsp paprika
- 400g cauliflower florets

Directions:

1. Preheat air fryer to 200ºC
2. Crush the garlic, place all ingredients in a bowl and mix well
3. Place in the air fryer and cook for about 15 minutes, shaking every 5 minutes

Falafel Burgers

Servings: 2

Ingredients:

- 1 large can of chickpeas
- 1 onion
- 1 lemon
- 140g oats
- 28g grated cheese
- 28g feta cheese
- Salt and pepper to taste
- 3 tbsp Greek yogurt
- 4 tbsp soft cheese
- 1 tbsp garlic puree
- 1 tbsp coriander
- 1 tbsp oregano
- 1 tbsp parsley

Directions:

1. Place the chickpeas, onion, lemon rind, garlic and seasonings and blend until coarse
2. Add the mix to a bowl and stir in half the soft cheese, cheese and feta
3. Form in to burger shape and coat in the oats
4. Place in the air fryer and cook at 180ºC for 8 minutes
5. To make the sauce mix the remaining soft cheese, greek yogurt and lemon juice in a bowl

Air Fryer Roasted Garlic

Servings: 4
Cooking Time: 20 Mints
Ingredients:

- 1 head garlic
- aluminum foil
- 1 teaspoon extra-virgin olive oil
- ¼ teaspoon salt
- ¼ teaspoon ground black pepper

Directions:

1. Preheat the air fryer to 190°C/375°F.
2. Cut the top off the head of garlic and place on a square piece of aluminum foil. Bring the foil up and around garlic. Pour olive oil on top and season with salt and pepper. Close ends of foil over garlic, creating a pouch.
3. Air fry until garlic is soft, 16 to 20 minutes. Open the foil pouch very carefully, as hot steam will escape.

Whole Wheat Pizza

Servings: 2
Ingredients:

- 100g marinara sauce
- 2 whole wheat pitta
- 200g baby spinach leaves
- 1 small plum tomato, sliced
- 1 clove garlic, sliced
- 400g grated cheese
- 50g shaved parmesan

Directions:

1. Preheat air fryer to 160°C
2. Spread each of the pitta with marinara sauce
3. Sprinkle with cheese, top with spinach, plum tomato and garlic. Finish with parmesan shavings
4. Place in the air fryer and cook for about 4 mins cheese has melted

Roasted Brussels Sprouts

Servings: 3

Ingredients:

- 300 g/10½ oz. Brussels sprouts, trimmed and halved
- 1 tablespoon olive oil
- ½ teaspoon salt
- ¼ teaspoon freshly ground black pepper

Directions:

1. Preheat the air-fryer to 160°C/325°F.
2. Toss the Brussels sprout halves in the oil and the seasoning. Add these to the preheated air-fryer and air-fry for 15 minutes, then increase the temperature of the air-fryer to 180°C/350°F and cook for a further 5 minutes until the sprouts are really crispy on the outside and cooked through.

Air Fryer Roasted Tomatoes

Servings: 4

Cooking Time: 20 Mints

Ingredients:

- 8-10 tomatoes
- 15 ml vegetable oil
- 4 cloves of garlic (leave the skin on!)
- 10 sprigs of thyme
- 1 sprig of rosemary
- Generous pinch of salt and pepper

Directions:

1. Wash and dry tomatoes.
2. Place in a bowl with the vegetable oil and garlic cloves.
3. Mix well until all tomatoes are coated.
4. Add the herbs and salt and pepper.
5. Cook at 200°C/400°F for 20 minutes. Check at the 10 minute mark and shake gently if needed

Air Fryer Green Beans

Servings: 2
Cooking Time: 10 Mints
Ingredients:

- 80 g of green beans per person
- Spray oil
- Salt and pepper

Directions:
1. Add to a bowl.
2. Use a few sprays of spray oil.
3. Add salt and pepper.
4. Toss gently to ensure even coverage.
5. Pre-heat your air fryer to 200°C/400°F.
6. Add the green beans to the air fryer basket.
7. Cook for 6 minutes. Stir at least once during cooking.

Baked Feta, Tomato & Garlic Pasta

Servings: 2
Ingredients:

- 100 g/3½ oz. feta or plant-based feta, cubed
- 20 cherry tomatoes
- 2 garlic cloves, peeled and halved
- ¾ teaspoon oregano
- 1 teaspoon chilli/hot red pepper flakes
- ½ teaspoon garlic salt
- 2 tablespoons olive oil
- 100 g/3½ oz. cooked pasta plus about 1 tablespoon of cooking water
- freshly ground black pepper

Directions:
1. Preheat the air-fryer to 200ºC/400ºF.
2. Place the feta, tomatoes and garlic in a baking dish that fits inside your air-fryer. Top with the oregano, chilli/hot red pepper flakes, garlic salt and olive oil. Place the dish in the preheated air-fryer and air-fry for 10 minutes, then remove and stir in the pasta and cooking water. Serve sprinkled with black pepper.

Tempura Veggies

Servings: 4

Ingredients:

- 150g flour
- ½ tsp salt
- ½ tsp pepper
- 2 eggs
- 2 tbsp cup water
- 100g avocado wedges
- 100g courgette slices
- 100g panko breadcrumbs
- 2 tsp oil
- 100g green beans
- 100g asparagus spears
- 100g red onion rings
- 100g pepper rings

Directions:

1. Mix together flour, salt and pepper. In another bowl mix eggs and water
2. Stir together panko crumbs and oil in a separate bowl
3. Dip vegetables in the flour mix, then egg and then the bread crumbs
4. Preheat the air fryer to 200ºC
5. Place in the air fryer and cook for about 10 minutes until golden brown

Roasted Vegetable Pasta

Servings:4
Cooking Time:15 Minutes
Ingredients:

- 400 g / 14 oz penne pasta
- 1 courgette, sliced
- 1 red pepper, deseeded and sliced
- 100 g / 3.5 oz mushroom, sliced
- 2 tbsp olive oil
- 1 tsp Italian seasoning
- 200 g cherry tomatoes, halved
- 2 tbsp fresh basil, chopped
- ½ tsp black pepper

Directions:

1. Cook the pasta according to the packet instructions.
2. Preheat the air fryer to 190 °C / 370 °F and line the air fryer with parchment paper or grease it with olive oil.
3. In a bowl, place the courgette, pepper, and mushroom, and toss in 2 tbsp olive oil
4. Place the vegetables in the air fryer and cook for 15 minutes.
5. Once the vegetables have softened, mix with the penne pasta, chopped cherry tomatoes, and fresh basil.
6. Serve while hot with a sprinkle of black pepper in each dish.

Buffalo Cauliflower Bites

Servings: 4
Ingredients:

- 3 tbsp ketchup
- 2 tbsp hot sauce
- 1 large egg white
- 200g panko bread crumbs
- 400g cauliflower
- ¼ tsp black pepper
- Cooking spray
- 40g sour cream
- 40g blue cheese
- 1 garlic clove, grated
- 1 tsp red wine vinegar

Directions:

1. Whisk together ketchup, hot sauce and egg white
2. Place the breadcrumbs in another bowl
3. Dip the cauliflower in the sauce then in the breadcrumbs
4. Coat with cooking spray
5. Place in the air fryer and cook at 160ºC for about 20 minutes until crispy
6. Mix remaining ingredients together and serve as a dip

Chickpea Falafel

Servings: 2

Ingredients:

- 400-g/14-oz can chickpeas, drained and rinsed
- 3 tablespoons freshly chopped coriander/cilantro
- 1 plump garlic clove, chopped
- freshly squeezed juice of ½ a lemon
- 1 teaspoon ground cumin
- 1 teaspoon smoked paprika
- 1 teaspoon salt
- 2 teaspoons olive oil (plus extra in a spray bottle or simply drizzle over)
- ½ teaspoon chilli/hot red pepper flakes

Directions:

1. In a food processor combine all the ingredients except the chilli/hot red pepper flakes. Divide the mixture into 6 equal portions and mould into patties.
2. Preheat the air-fryer to 180ºC/350ºF.
3. Spray each falafel with extra olive oil and sprinkle with chilli/hot red pepper flakes, then place in the preheated air-fryer and air-fry for 7 minutes, or until just brown on top. Remove carefully and serve.

Ratatouille

Servings: 4

Ingredients:

- ½ small aubergine, cubed
- 1 courgette, cubed
- 1 tomato, cubed
- 1 pepper, cut into cubes
- ½ onion, diced
- 1 fresh cayenne pepper, sliced
- 1 tsp vinegar
- 5 sprigs basil, chopped
- 2 sprigs oregano, chopped
- 1 clove garlic, crushed
- Salt and pepper
- 1 tbsp olive oil
- 1 tbsp white wine

Directions:

1. Preheat air fryer to 200ºC
2. Place all ingredients in a bowl and mix
3. Pour into a baking dish
4. Add dish to the air fryer and cook for 8 minutes, stir then cook for another 10 minutes

Orange Zingy Cauliflower

Servings: 2

Ingredients:

- 200ml water
- 200g flour
- Half the head of a cauliflower, cut into 1.5" florets
- 2 tsp olive oil
- 2 minced garlic cloves
- 1 tsp minced ginger
- 150ml orange juice
- 3 tbsp white vinegar
- 1/2 tsp red pepper flakes
- 1 tsp sesame oil 100g brown sugar
- 3 tbsp soy sauce
- 1 tbsp cornstarch
- 2 tbsp water
- 1 tsp salt

Directions:

1. Take a medium mixing bowl and add the water, salt and flour together
2. Dip each floret of cauliflower into the mixture and place in the air fryer basket
3. Cook at 220ºC for 15 minutes
4. Meanwhile make the orange sauce by combining all ingredients in a saucepan and allowing to simmer for 3 minutes, until the sauce has thickened
5. Drizzle the sauce over the cauliflower to serve

Vegetarian Air Fryer Kimchi Bun

Servings: 4

Cooking Time: 20 Mints

Ingredients:

- 1300 g pack of Quorn Mince
- 1/2 cup chopped kimchi, save a splash of kimchi juice
- 2-3 chopped spring onions
- 1 egg
- 1 tbsp sesame oil
- 1 tbsp soy sauce
- 1 tsp white pepper powder
- Pinch of salt
- For the dough:
- 480 g flour
- 260 ml warm water
- 2 g salt

Directions:

1. Combine all the dough ingredients in a large bowl, mix well and shape into a ball. Let the dough rest for 10 minutes before kneading for 5 minutes and then resting for a further hour.

2. Mix all the remaining ingredients together, ensuring all liquid has been well absorbed by the Quorn Mince.

3. Lay out the dough on a lightly floured surface and cut into 16 equal pieces (about 30g/piece).

4. Wrap an equal amount of filling into each piece of dough, using your hands to form into a smooth and tightly wrapped bun.

5. Preheat air fryer to 180°C/350°F Place the buns into the air fryer and spray some oil over the top of each bun, cook for 10-15 mins until golden and enjoy!

Desserts Recipes
New York Cheesecake

Servings: 8

Ingredients:

- 225g plain flour
- 100g brown sugar
- 100g butter
- 50g melted butter
- 1 tbsp vanilla essence
- 750g soft cheese
- 2 cups caster sugar
- 3 large eggs
- 50ml quark

Directions:

1. Add the flour, sugar, and 100g butter to a bowl and mix until combined. Form into biscuit shapes place in the air fryer and cook for 15 minutes at 180°C
2. Grease a springform tin
3. Break the biscuits up and mix with the melted butter, press firmly into the tin
4. Mix the soft cheese and sugar in a bowl until creamy, add the eggs and vanilla and mix. Mix in the quark
5. Pour the cheesecake batter into the pan
6. Place in your air fryer and cook for 30 minutes at 180°C. Leave in the air fryer for 30 minutes whilst it cools
7. Refrigerate for 6 hours

Apple And Cinnamon Empanadas

Servings: 12

Ingredients:

- 12 empanada wraps
- 2 diced apples
- 2 tbsp honey
- 1 tsp vanilla extract
- 1 tsp cinnamon
- ⅛ tsp nutmeg
- Olive oil spray
- 2 tsp cornstarch
- 1 tsp water

Directions:

1. Place apples, cinnamon, honey, vanilla and nutmeg in a pan cook for 2-3 minutes until apples are soft
2. Mix the cornstarch and water add to the pan and cook for 30 seconds
3. Add the apple mix to each of the empanada wraps
4. Roll the wrap in half, pinch along the edges, fold the edges in then continue to roll to seal
5. Place in the air fryer and cook at 200°C for 8 minutes, turn and cook for another 10 minutes

Strawberry Danish

Servings: 2

Ingredients:

- 1 tube crescent roll dough
- 200g cream cheese
- 25g strawberry jam
- 50g diced strawberries
- 225g powdered sugar
- 2-3 tbsp cream

Directions:

1. Roll out the dough
2. Spread the cream cheese over the dough, cover in jam
3. Sprinkle with strawberries
4. Roll the dough up from the short side and pinch to seal
5. Line the air fryer with parchment paper and spray with cooking spray
6. Place the dough in the air fryer and cook at 175°C for 20 minutes
7. Mix the cream with the powdered sugar and drizzle on top once cooked

White Chocolate Pudding

Servings:2

Cooking Time:15 Minutes

Ingredients:

- 100 g / 3.5 oz white chocolate
- 50 g brown sugar
- 2 tbsp olive oil
- ½ tsp vanilla extract
- 4 egg whites, plus two egg yolks

Directions:

1. Preheat the air fryer to 180 °C / 350 °F and line the mesh basket with parchment paper or grease it with olive oil.
2. Place the white chocolate in a saucepan and place it over low heat until it melts, being careful not to let the chocolate burn.
3. Stir in the brown sugar, olive oil, and vanilla extract.
4. Whisk the egg whites and egg yolks in a bowl until well combined. Fold a third of the eggs into the white chocolate mixture and stir until it forms a smooth and consistent mixture. Repeat twice more with the other two-thirds of the eggs.
5. Pour the white chocolate pudding mixture evenly into two ramekins and place the ramekins in the lined air fryer basket. Cook for 15 minutes until the pudding is hot and set on top.

Grilled Ginger & Coconut Pineapple Rings

Servings: 4

Ingredients:

- 1 medium pineapple
- coconut oil, melted
- 1½ teaspoons coconut sugar
- ½ teaspoon ground ginger
- coconut or vanilla yogurt, to serve

Directions:

1. Preheat the air-fryer to 180ºC/350ºF.
2. Peel and core the pineapple, then slice into 4 thick rings.
3. Mix together the melted coconut oil with the sugar and ginger in a small bowl. Using a pastry brush, paint this mixture all over the pineapple rings, including the sides of the rings.
4. Add the rings to the preheated air-fryer and air-fry for 20 minutes. Check after 18 minutes as pineapple sizes vary and your rings may be perfectly cooked already. You'll know they are ready when they're golden in colour and a fork can easily be inserted with very little resistance
5. Serve warm with a generous spoonful of yogurt.

Profiteroles

Servings: 9

Ingredients:

- 100g butter
- 200g plain flour
- 6 eggs
- 300ml water
- 2 tsp vanilla extract
- 300ml whipped cream
- 100g milk chocolate
- 2 tbsp whipped cream
- 50g butter
- 2 tsp icing sugar

Directions:

1. Preheat the air fryer to 170ºC
2. Place the butter and water in a pan over a medium heat, bring to the boil, remove from the heat and stir in the flour
3. Return to the heat stirring until a dough is formed
4. Mix in the eggs and stir until mixture is smooth, make into profiterole shapes and cook in the air fryer for 10 minutes
5. For the filling whisk together 300ml whipped cream, vanilla extract and the icing sugar
6. For the topping place the butter, 2tbsp whipped cream and chocolate in a bowl and melt over a pan of hot water until mixed together
7. Pipe the filling into the roles and finish off with a chocolate topping

Butter Cake

Servings: 4

Ingredients:

- Cooking spray
- 7 tbsp butter
- 25g white sugar
- 2 tbsp white sugar
- 1 egg
- 300g flour
- Pinch salt
- 6 tbsp milk

Directions:

1. Preheat air fryer to 175°C
2. Spray a small fluted tube pan with cooking spray
3. Beat the butter and all of the sugar together in a bowl until creamy
4. Add the egg and mix until fluffy, add the salt and flour mix well. Add the milk and mix well
5. Put the mix in the pan and cook in the air fryer for 15 minutes

Apple Pie

Servings: 2

Ingredients:

- 1 packet of ready made pastry
- 1 apple, chopped
- 2 tsp lemon juice
- 1 tsp cinnamon
- 2 tbsp sugar
- ½ tsp vanilla extract
- 1 tbsp butter
- 1 beaten egg
- 1 tbsp raw sugar

Directions:

1. Preheat the air fryer to 160°C
2. Line a baking tin with pastry
3. Mix the apple, lemon juice, cinnamon, sugar and vanilla in a bowl
4. Pour the apple mix into the tin with the pastry, top with chunks of butter
5. Cover with a second piece of pastry, place three slits in the top of the pastry
6. Brush the pastry with beaten egg and sprinkle with raw sugar
7. Place in the air fryer and cook for 30 minutes

Special Oreos

Servings: 9

Ingredients:

- 100g pancake mix
- 25ml water
- Cooking spray
- 9 Oreos
- 1 tbsp icing sugar

Directions:

1. Mix pancake mix and water until well combined
2. Line the air fryer with parchment paper and spray with cooking spray
3. Preheat the air fryer to 200ºC
4. Dip each cookie in the pancake mix and place in the air fryer
5. Cook for 5 minutes, turn and cook for a further 3 minutes
6. Sprinkle with icing sugar to serve

Birthday Cheesecake

Servings: 8

Ingredients:

- 6 Digestive biscuits
- 50g melted butter
- 800g soft cheese
- 500g caster sugar
- 4 tbsp cocoa powder
- 6 eggs
- 2 tbsp honey
- 1 tbsp vanilla

Directions:

1. Flour a spring form tin to prevent sticking
2. Crush the biscuits and then mix with the melted butter, press into the bottom and sides of the tin
3. Mix the caster sugar and soft cheese with an electric mixer. Add 5 eggs, honey and vanilla. Mix well
4. Spoon half the mix into the pan and pat down well. Place in the air fryer and cook at 180ºC for 20 minutes then 160ºC for 15 minutes and then 150ºC for 20 minutes
5. Mix the cocoa and the last egg into the remaining mix. Spoon over the over the bottom layer and place in the fridge. Chill for 11 hours

Banana Cake

Servings: 4

Ingredients:

- Cooking spray
- 25g brown sugar
- ½ tbsp butter
- 1 banana, mashed
- 1 egg
- 2 tbsp honey
- 225g self raising flour
- ½ tsp cinnamon
- Pinch salt

Directions:

1. Preheat air fryer to 160°C
2. Spray a small fluted tube tray with cooking spray
3. Beat sugar and butter together in a bowl until creamy
4. Combine the banana egg and honey together in another bowl
5. Mix into the butter until smooth
6. Sift in the remaining ingredients and mix well
7. Spoon into the tray and cook in the air fryer for 30 minutes

Apple Fritters

Servings: 4

Ingredients:

- 225g self raising flour
- 200g greek yogurt
- 2 tsp sugar
- 1 tbsp cinnamon
- 1 apple peeled and chopped
- 225g icing sugar
- 2 tbsp milk

Directions:

1. Mix the flour, yogurt, sugar, cinnamon and apple together. Knead for about 3 -4 minutes
2. Mix the icing sugar and milk together to make the glaze and set aside
3. Line the air fryer with parchment paper and spray with cooking spray
4. Divide the fritter mix into four, flatten each portion and place in the air fryer
5. Cook at 185°C for about 15 minutes turning halfway
6. Drizzle with glaze to serve

Peach Pies(2)

Servings: 8

Ingredients:

- 2 peaches, peeled and chopped
- 1 tbsp lemon juice
- 3 tbsp sugar
- 1 tsp vanilla extract
- ¼ tsp salt
- 1 tsp cornstarch
- 1 pack ready made pastry
- Cooking spray

Directions:

1. Mix together peaches, lemon juice, sugar and vanilla in a bowl. Stand for 15 minutes
2. Drain the peaches keeping 1 tbsp of the liquid, mix cornstarch into the peaches
3. Cut the pastry into 8 circles, fill with the peach mix
4. Brush the edges of the pastry with water and fold over to form half moons, crimp the edges to seal
5. Coat with cooking spray
6. Add to the air fryer and cook at 170ºC for 12 minutes until golden brown

Baked Nectarines

Servings: 4

Ingredients:

- 2 teaspoons maple syrup
- 1 teaspoon vanilla extract
- 1 teaspoon ground cinnamon
- 4 nectarines, halved and stones/pits removed
- chopped nuts, yogurt and runny honey, to serve (optional)

Directions:

1. Preheat the air-fryer to 180ºC/350º F.

2. Mix the maple syrup, vanilla extract and cinnamon in a ramekin or shake in a jar to combine. Lay the nectarine halves on an air-fryer liner or piece of pierced parchment paper. Drizzle over the maple syrup mix.

3. Place in the preheated air-fryer and air-fry for 9–11 minutes, until soft when pricked with a fork. Serve scattered with chopped nuts and with a generous dollop of yogurt. Drizzle over some honey if you wish.

Christmas Biscuits

Servings: 8

Ingredients:

- 225g self raising flour
- 100g caster sugar
- 100g butter
- Juice and rind of orange
- 1 egg beaten
- 2 tbsp cocoa
- 2 tsp vanilla essence
- 8 pieces dark chocolate

Directions:

1. Preheat the air fryer to 180ºC
2. Rub the butter into the flour. Add the sugar, vanilla, orange and cocoa mix well
3. Add the egg and mix to a dough
4. Split the dough into 8 equal pieces
5. Place a piece of chocolate in each piece of dough and form into a ball covering the chocolate
6. Place in the air fryer and cook for 15 minutes

Pecan & Molasses Flapjack

Servings:9

Ingredients:

- 120 g/½ cup plus 2 teaspoons butter or plant-based spread, plus extra for greasing
- 40 g/2 tablespoons blackstrap molasses
- 60 g/5 tablespoons unrefined sugar
- 50 g/½ cup chopped pecans
- 200 g/1½ cups porridge oats/steelcut oats (not rolled or jumbo)

Directions:

1. Preheat the air-fryer to 180ºC/350ºF.
2. Grease and line a 15 x 15-cm/6 x 6-in. baking pan.
3. In a large saucepan melt the butter/spread, molasses and sugar. Once melted, stir in the pecans, then the oats. As soon as they are combined, tip the mixture into the prepared baking pan and cover with foil.
4. Place the foil-covered baking pan in the preheated air-fryer and air-fry for 10 minutes. Remove the foil, then cook for a further 2 minutes to brown the top. Leave to cool, then cut into 9 squares.

White Chocolate And Raspberry Loaf

Servings:8

Cooking Time:1 Hour 10 Minutes

Ingredients:

- 400 g / 14 oz plain flour
- 2 tsp baking powder
- 1 tsp ground cinnamon
- ½ tsp salt
- 3 eggs, beaten
- 50 g / 3.5 oz granulated sugar
- 50 g / 3.5 oz brown sugar
- 100 g / 3.5 oz white chocolate chips
- 100 g / 3.5 oz fresh raspberries
- 1 tbsp cocoa powder
- 4 tbsp milk
- 1 tsp vanilla extract

Directions:

1. Preheat the air fryer to 150 °C / 300 °F and line a loaf tin with parchment paper.
2. Combine the plain flour, baking powder, ground cinnamon, and salt in a large mixing bowl.
3. Whisk eggs into the bowl, then stir in the granulated sugar and brown sugar. Mix well before folding in the white chocolate chips, fresh raspberries, cocoa powder, milk, and vanilla extract.
4. Stir the mixture until it is lump-free and transfer into a lined loaf tin. Place the loaf tin into the lined air fryer basket, close the lid, and cook for 30-40 minutes.
5. The cake should be golden and set by the end of the cooking process. Insert a knife into the centre of the cake. It should come out dry when the cake is fully cooked.
6. Remove the cake from the air fryer, still in the loaf tin. Set aside to cool on a drying rack for 20-30 minutes before cutting into slices and serving.

Brazilian Pineapple

Servings: 2

Ingredients:

- 1 small pineapple, cut into spears
- 100g brown sugar
- 2 tsp cinnamon
- 3 tbsp melted butter

Directions:

1. Mix the brown sugar and cinnamon together in a small bowl
2. Brush the pineapple with melted butter
3. Sprinkle with the sugar and cinnamon
4. Heat the air fryer to 200ºC
5. Cook the pineapple for about 10 minutes

Lemon Pies

Servings: 6

Ingredients:

- 1 pack of pastry
- 1 egg beaten
- 200g lemon curd
- 225g powdered sugar
- ½ lemon

Directions:

1. Preheat the air fryer to 180ºC
2. Cut out 6 circles from the pastry using a cookie cutter
3. Add 1 tbsp of lemon curd to each circle, brush the edges with egg and fold over
4. Press around the edges of the dough with a fork to seal
5. Brush the pies with the egg and cook in the air fryer for 10 minutes
6. Mix the lemon juice with the powdered sugar to make the icing and drizzle on the cooked pies

Lemon Buns

Servings: 12

Ingredients:

- 100g butter
- 100g caster sugar
- 2 eggs
- 100g self raising flour
- ½ tsp vanilla essence
- 1 tsp cherries
- 50g butter
- 100g icing sugar
- ½ small lemon rind and juice

Directions:

1. Preheat the air fryer to 170ºC
2. Cream the 100g butter, sugar and vanilla together until light and fluffy
3. Beat in the eggs one at a time adding a little flour with each
4. Fold in the remaining flour
5. Half fill bun cases with the mix, place in the air fryer and cook for 8 minutes
6. Cream 50g butter then mix in the icing sugar, stir in the lemon
7. Slice the top off each bun and create a butterfly shape using the icing to hold together. Add a 1/3 cherry to each one

Cinnamon Biscuit Bites

Servings: 16

Ingredients:

- 200g flour
- 200g wholewheat flour
- 2 tbsp sugar
- 1 tsp baking powder
- ¼ tsp cinnamon
- ¼ tsp salt
- 4 tbsp butter
- 50ml milk
- Cooking spray
- 300g icing sugar
- 3 tbsp water

Directions:

1. Mix together flour, salt, sugar baking powder and cinnamon in a bowl
2. Add butter and mix until well combined
3. Add milk and form a dough, place dough on a floured surface and knead until smooth
4. Cut into 16 equal pieces and form each piece into a ball
5. Place in the air fryer and cook at 180°C for about 12 minutes
6. Mix together icing sugar and water and coat to serve

Recipe Index

Panko-crusted Air Fryer Mahi Mahi 57

Pepper & Lemon Chicken Wings 35

Peppery Lemon Shrimp 62

Pesto Salmon 60

Peach Pies(2) 96

Pecan & Molasses Flapjack 97

Pork Schnitzel 52

Potato Wedges 69

Potato Wedges With Rosemary 72

Q

Quick Chicken Nuggets 35

R

Ratatouille 87

Ricotta Stuffed Aubergine 73

Roasted Brussels Sprouts 83

Roasted Garlic 77

Roasted Vegetable Pasta 86

Roasted Cauliflower 81

S

Shrimp With Yum Yum Sauce 59

Shishito Peppers 71

Spring Rolls 25

Special Oreos 94

Spicy Chicken Wing Drummettes 33

Strawberry Danish 91

Steak And Mushrooms 51

Sticky Asian Beef 48

Super Easy Fries 69

Sweet Potato Wedges 67

Sweet Potato Crisps 28

Sweet And Sticky Parsnips And Carrots 71

Salmon Patties 58

Satay Chicken Skewers 36

Sausage Gnocchi One Pot 54

Simple Steaks 46

T

Thai Fish Cakes 56

Traditional Pork Chops 52

Turkey And Mushroom Burgers 33

Tasty Pumpkin Seeds 27

Tempura Veggies 85

Tortellini Bites 23

V

Vegetarian Air Fryer Kimchi Bun 89

W

White Chocolate Pudding 91

White Chocolate And Raspberry Loaf 98

Whole Wheat Pizza 82

Wholegrain Pitta Chips 18

Y

Your Favourite Breakfast Bacon 16

Printed in Great Britain
by Amazon

41169688R00057